Leaping Over the Caudine of Capitalism

In the four volumes of *The Development Trajectory of Eastern Societies and the Theories and Practices of Socialism*, the author re-examines Marx and Engels' theories on the development trajectory of Eastern societies by integrating theoretical analysis of Marxist theories and a historical investigation of socialist revolution and construction around the world.

This volume discusses the desire of the Russian commune to "leap over the Caudine Forks of capitalism," which means to avoid the torments of the capitalist system, according to Marx and Engels' theories. The author argues that it is essential to use the logic intrinsic in Marx and Engels' own works rather than those of subsequent disciples such as Lenin as well as other leaders in the Soviet Union or within China's contemporary socialism.

Readers who study Marxism, Marxist philosophy, philosophical history, and the history of philosophy will find this volume interesting.

Jiaxiang Zhao is Professor of Philosophy at Peking University, and has served as vice dean, professor, and director of the academic committee of the Department of Philosophy, as well as vice president and consultant of the Chinese Historical Materialism Association. His main research interests include Marxist philosophy and Marxist classic works.

China Perspectives

The *China Perspectives* series focuses on translating and publishing works by leading Chinese scholars, writing about both global topics and China-related themes. It covers Humanities & Social Sciences, Education, Media and Psychology, as well as many interdisciplinary themes.

This is the first time any of these books have been published in English for international readers. The series aims to put forward a Chinese perspective, give insights into cutting-edge academic thinking in China, and inspire researchers globally.

Titles in philosophy currently include:

Explanation, Laws, and Causation
Wang Wei

Secret Subversion I
Mou Zongsan, Kant, and Original Confucianism
Wenming Tang

Secret Subversion II
Mou Zongsan, Kant, and Original Confucianism
Wenming Tang

The Development Trajectory of Eastern Societies
Jiaxiang Zhao

Historical Evolution of the Eastern Mode of Production
Jiaxiang Zhao

Leaping Over the Caudine Forks of Capitalism
Jiaxiang Zhao

Theories and Practices of Scientific Socialism
Jiaxiang Zhao

The Principles of New Ethics
Volume 3: Normative Ethics II
Haiming Wang

For more information, please visit https://www.routledge.com/series/CPH

Leaping Over the Caudine Forks of Capitalism

Jiaxiang Zhao

Translated by Qin Li

Routledge
Taylor & Francis Group
LONDON AND NEW YORK

First published 2021 by Routledge

2 Park Square, Milton Park, Abingdon, Oxon OX14 4RN
605 Third Avenue, New York, NY 10017

Routledge is an imprint of the Taylor & Francis Group, an informa business

First issued in paperback 2022

Translated by Qin Li

Publisher's Note

The publisher has gone to great lengths to ensure the quality of this reprint but points out that some imperfections in the original copies may be apparent.

English version by permission of The Commercial Press.

British Library Cataloguing-in-Publication Data
A catalogue record for this book is available from the British Library

Library of Congress Cataloging-in-Publication Data
A catalog record has been requested for this book

ISBN: 978-0-367-47846-9 (hbk)
ISBN: 978-1-03-233606-0 (pbk)
DOI: 10.4324/9781003036869

Typeset in Times New Roman
by Deanta Global Publishing Services, Chennai, India

The Commercial Press

Contents

Introduction

During the second Samnite war in 321 BC, the Samnites besieged and defeated the Roman army at Caudine Forks near Caudine (now Montesalchio) in Rome. In accordance with the practice of Italians, the Roman army must go beneath an "archway" formed by crossed spears. This was considered a high humiliation for the defeated army. That was the origin of the phrase "go through the Caudine Forks", meaning suffering through a grotesque humiliation. In the first and third drafts of his letter to Vera Zasulich, Marx said: The Russian commune "may therefore incorporate the positive achievements developed by the capitalist system, without having to pass under its harsh tribute."[1] Here "without having to pass under its harsh tribute" means without having to go through the blight of capitalism. "Leaping over the Caudine Forks of capitalism" in the chapter means without passing through the torments of the capitalist system. The use of "leaping over" instead of "without passing through" is for sake of brevity.

Marx and Engels' thought on the Russian commune's possibility to "leap over" the Caudine Forks of capitalism was a "hot topic" in Chinese academia since mid-1980s. Many books and articles have appeared on the topic. Much controversy remains. Scholars have offered great explanations and interpretations of Marx and Engels. Others have very much misunderstood Marx and Engels. I will not dwell on every particularity of the controversy but will instead focus on prominent misinterpretations of Marx and Engels as a way to invite further discussion from my scholarly peers. To properly understand Marx and Engels on the issue, we should use logic intrinsic within their own works rather than those by subsequent disciples of Marx such as Lenin; In addition, we should not use historical conditions outside the purview of Marx and Engels—such as those in the Soviet Union or in China's contemporary socialism.

Note

1 *Collected Works of Marx and Engels* (Vol. 3). (2009). Beijing, China: People's Publishing House, 575, 578, 587.

1   The nature and prospect of Russian communes

The nature and evolution of the Russian commune are complex and controversial issues. One prevalent traditional view deems the commune a "legacy" of ancient primitive communes. However, since the late 1970s and early 1980s, some scholars in the Soviet Union stepped outside traditional theories. For example, Alaev and Alekseyev proposed that rural communes were established to cement authoritarian centralization rather than being vestigial manifestations of primitive communes. The idea that the rural commune was preceded by private ownership rather than by primitive public ownership was indirectly supported by the Leningrad School (e.g., Frojanov in the 1980s). This school argued that before the era of authoritarianism, a classical civil society existed in Russia. The controversy aroused intense criticism from most scholars and academic authorities in the Soviet Union. To some extent, this controversy replicates the debate between the "Slavic School" and the "Western School" in the 19th century on the "natural relic theory" and the "state creation theory" of rural communes.[1] Marx paid close attention to the debate and offered his opinions. He disapproved of the "state creation theory." In his letter to Nikolai Danielson on March 22, 1873, Marx questioned the views of Chechilin, representative of the "state creation theory." Marx said:

> This system [the communal ownership of land-author] is naturally produced in all other countries and is an inevitable stage in the development of various free nations. How can this system be implemented purely as a state measure and as a concomitant phenomenon of serfdom in Russia?[2]

The nature, emergence, and evolution of the Russian commune are not the subject of this book. The rights and wrongs of this issue are not assessed in this book. Without deep nuanced research, the author is unable to render proper judgments. This book focuses on the thoughts of Marx and Engels on the issue. Whether their views conform to objective historical facts or not presents no hindrance to our effort to understand Marx and Engels' thoughts on this issue.

1.1 The nature of the Russian commune and its two possible prospects

On the nature of Russian commune, Marx said in the first draft of his letter to Vera Zasulich in 1881:

> Accordingly, the "agricultural commune" everywhere presents itself as the *most recent type* of the archaic formation of societies; and the period of the agricultural commune appears in the historical course of Western Europe, both ancient and modern, as a period of transition from communal to private property, from the primary to the secondary formation.[3]

Marx also described the emergence and evolution of the German commune:

> We know nothing of the life of the [Germanic] [rural] [archaic] *commune* after Tacitus, nor how and when it actually disappeared. Thanks to Julius Caesar, however, we do at least know its point of departure. In Caesar's time, the [arable] land was already distributed on an annual basis—not yet, however, among individual members of a commune, but among the *gentes* [Geschlechter] and tribes of the [various] Germanic confederations. The *agricultural rural commune* therefore emerged in Germania from a more archaic type; it was the product of spontaneous development rather than being imported ready-made from Asia. It may also be found in Asia—in the East Indies—always as *the final term* or last period of the archaic formation.[4]

Based on their studies of the rural communes in Germania and India, Marx regarded the rural communes in all countries (including Russia) largely the same in nature and evolution. He said:

> As [the most recent and] the latest phase in the [archaic] primitive formation of society, the agrarian commune [which naturally represents the transition] is at the same time a phase in the transition to the secondary formation, and therefore in the transition from a society based on communal property to one based on private property. The secondary formation does, of course, include the series of societies which rest upon slavery and serfdom.[5]

That is, Marx clearly affirmed the Russian rural commune as the final stage of the primitive society, a stage transitional from the primary to a secondary formation, from a public to a private system, and from the classless to a class society.

Being a transitional stage, the Russian commune had a "duality" of public and private ownership, and of a classless and class society. Its characteristics differed from those of a primitive commune, as largely manifested in the following three aspects. First, earlier primitive communes all rested on the natural kinship of their members. In breaking this strong yet narrow tie, the agricultural rural commune proved more capable of expanding its scope and maintaining contact with other communes. Second, within the commune, the house and its appended yard were already the farmer's private property, whereas the communal house of previous primitive communities was one of the material bases of the latter, long before agriculture was even introduced. Finally, arable land, though remaining as communal property, was periodically divided among members of the agricultural commune, so that each farmer tilled the fields allocated to him and individually appropriated the fruits of their labor. In the more archaic communities, by contrast, production was a communal activity, and the final produce was shared among individual members. Of course, this primitive communal production stemmed from the weakness of the isolated individual, not from socialization of the means of production.

Marx believed that the "dualism" inherent in the Russian "agricultural commune" may give it a sturdy life on one hand, but on the other hand may be the ultimate anathema of the agricultural commune. Concerning the former, Marx said,

> It is easy to see that the dualism inherent in the "agricultural commune" may give it a sturdy life: for communal property and all the resulting social relations provide it with a solid foundation, while the privately owned houses, fragmented tillage of the arable land and private appropriation of its fruits all permit a development of individuality incompatible with conditions in the more primitive communities.

With regard to the latter, Marx offered this analysis,

> Apart from the influence of a hostile environment, the mere accumulation over time of movable property, beginning with wealth in livestock and even extending to wealth in serfs, combines with the ever more prominent role played by movables in agriculture itself and with a host of other circumstances, inseparable from such accumulation, which would take me too far from the central theme. All these factors, then, serve to dissolve economic and social equality, generating within the commune itself a conflict of interests which leads, first, to the conversion of arable land into private property, and ultimately to the private appropriation of forests, pastures, waste ground, etc., already no more than communal appendages of private property.[6]

Marx was very concerned about and condemned the various factors and forces that had caused the collapse of the communes. In response to the 1861 serf reform, he said:

> After the so-called emancipation of the peasantry, the state placed the Russian commune in abnormal economic conditions; and since that time, it has never ceased to weigh it down with the social force concentrated in its hands. Exhausted by tax demands, the commune became a kind of inert matter easily exploited by traders, landowners and usurers. This oppression from without unleashed the conflict of interests already present at the heart of the

commune, rapidly developing the seeds of its disintegration. But that is not all. [At the peasant's expense, it grew as in a hothouse those excrescences of the capitalist system that can be most easily acclimatised (the stock exchange, speculation, banks, share companies, railways), writing off their deficits, advancing profits to their entrepreneurs, etc., etc.] At the peasant's expense, the state grew in hothouse conditions certain branches of the Western capitalist system which, in no way developing the productive premises of agriculture, are the best suited to facilitate and precipitate the theft of its fruits by unproductive middlemen. In this way, it helped to enrich a new capitalist vermin which is sucking the already depleted blood of the "rural commune."

He was clearly aware of the combination of various destructive influences, saying "unless it is broken by a powerful reaction, this combination of destructive influences must naturally lead to the death of the rural commune."[7]

Although Marx fully foresaw the crisis and even potential demise faced by the Russian rural commune, he did not believe that that was the only destiny of the commune. He believed that in the then-historical environment, Russian rural communes had another prospect—"leaping over the Caudine Forks of capitalism" to precipitate the Russian society into a new form.

1.2 The possibility and historical environment for achieving the "leaping over"

Marx comprehensively analyzed the possibility and historical environment for the Russian commune to "leap over" the Caudine Forks of capitalism. First of all, Russia was the only European country that still maintained rural communes across its land. Unlike the East Indies, Russia did not fall victim of foreign conquerors. Public ownership of land made it possible to directly and gradually transform smallholdings into collective farming, and Russian farmers had already carried out collective farming on pastures not in distribution. Russia had a vast plain, suitable for large agricultural machinery. Russian peasants had the habit of working together, which was conducive to their transition from a smallholding economy into a collective economy.

Second, contemporaneous with capitalism, the Russian rural commune may be able to incorporate the positive fruits of capitalism without having to endure its torments. It may exploit such fruits for a direct transformation into socialism. When Russia's "new pillars of society" who worshiped capitalism denied this possibility, Marx asserted sharply:

> Should the Russian admirers of the capitalist system deny that such a development is theoretically possible, then I would ask them the following question. Did Russia have to undergo a long Western-style incubation of mechanical industry before it could make use of machinery, steamships, railways, etc.? Let them also explain how they managed to introduce, in the twinkling of an eye, that whole machinery of exchange (banks, credit companies, etc.) which was the work of centuries in the West.[8]

Third, Russian rural commune was in a historical era when capitalism was in deep crisis and was to be replaced by socialism and communism. This could be the most fundamental social and historical condition for Russian rural commune to "leap over" the Caudine Forks of capitalism. Marx attached great importance to this condition. In the first draft of his letter to Vera Zasulich, Marx mentioned this idea three times. In order to highlight this idea and draw readers' attention to it, I have cited three original texts of Marx as follows:

> Also favourable to the maintenance of the Russian commune (through its further development) is the fact not only that it is contemporary with capitalist production [in the Western countries], but that it has survived the epoch when the social system stood intact. Today, it faces a social system which, both in Western Europe and the United States, is in conflict with science, with the popular masses, and with the very productive forces that it generates [in short, this social system has become the arena of flagrant antagonisms, conflicts and periodic disasters; it makes clear to the blindest observer that it is a transitory system of production, doomed to be eliminated as soc(iety) returns to…]. In short, the rural commune finds it in a state of crisis that will end only when the social system is eliminated through the return of modern societies to the 'archaic' type of communal property. In the words of an American writer who, supported in his work by the Washington government, is not at all to be suspected of revolutionary tendencies, ["the higher plane"] "the new system" to which modern society is tending "will be a revival, in a superior form, of an archaic social type."[9]
>
> Historically very favourable to the preservation of the "agricultural commune" through its further development is the fact not only that it is contemporaneous with Western capitalist production and therefore able to acquire its fruits without bowing to its modus operandi, but also that it has survived the epoch when the capitalist system stood intact. Today it finds that system, both in Western Europe and the United States, in conflict with the working masses, with science, and with the very productive forces which it generates – in short, in a crisis that will end through its own elimination, through the return of modern societies to a higher form of an "archaic" type of collective ownership and production.[10]
>
> The best proof that such a development of the "rural commune" corresponds to the historical trend of our epoch, is the fatal crisis undergone by capitalist production in those European and American countries where it reached its highest peak. The crisis will come to an end with the elimination of capitalist production and the return of modern society to a higher form of the most archaic type – collective production and appropriation.[11]

Many researchers in China have only noticed that Marx's condition for the Russian commune to "leap over" the Caudine Forks of capitalism is the commune's being contemporaneous with capitalism. These same researchers however ignored that at that time, capitalism was also in deep crisis, likely to be replaced by socialism and communism. In fact, being cotemporaneous with capitalism is not a sufficient condition for "leaping over" the Caudine Forks of capitalism. Only in an era when capitalism is declining and to be replaced by socialism and communism can the Russian commune "leap over" the Caudine Forks of capitalism. Therefore, to Marx, the proletarian victory in developed European and American capitalism is a prerequisite for the Russian commune to "leap over" the Caudine Forks of capitalism. This point will be further discussed below.

We have talked about the three conditions for the Russian commune to leap over the Caudine Forks of the capitalist system. The first is inherent in the domestic conditions of the Russian society and the Russian commune. The second and the third conditions were international and historical. Under its current domestic conditions, the possibility for the Russian commune to leap over the Caudine Forks of capitalism depended on the international and the historical contexts. Marx repeatedly emphasized this important thought. Marx pointed out:

> Its (the agricultural commune's) constitutive form allows of the following alternative: either the element of private property which it implies gains the upper hand over the collective element, or the reverse takes place. Everything depends upon the historical context in which it is situated ... Both solutions are a priori possibilities, but each one naturally requires a completely different historical context.[12]

Which of the two prospects the Russian commune would materialize would hinge upon the historical and international environments. If the proletarian revolution in the developed European and American capitalist countries had won, and the Russian rural commune would have stayed intact; the possibility of "leaping over" the Caudine Forks of capitalism would be realized. However, if the proletarian revolutions in Europe and America and other developed capitalist countries were delayed, the Russian rural commune would disintegrate and Russia would slide onto the capitalistic path.

Marx's thought offers great methodological significance. It tells us that when human history becomes international, the trajectory of a nation's development depends on both domestic and international conditions. The study of a country's development cannot be severed from its international environment. The victories of the Russian October Revolution and of the Chinese Revolution were achieved in a particular international context. The tragic disintegration of the Soviet Union and the upheavals in Eastern Europe also took place in a particular international context. China's reform and opening-up, together with the path, principles, and policies of its modernization drive, are based on both domestic and international environments.

Chinese academia debates whether the Russian rural commune or the entire Russian society was likely to leap over the Caudine Forks of capitalism. The possibility for both is the same to Marx and Engels, because in the 1870s and 1880s, both the Russian rural commune and the entire Russian society were precapitalistic and were both likely to "leap over" the Caudine Forks of capitalism.

If the Russian rural commune had embarked on the path of capitalism, so would the entire Russian society. In that case, neither would leap over the Caudine Forks of capitalism.

Incidentally, in the book *A Brief Introduction to Marxist Theory of Social Formations*, the author clearly distinguished between the Russian rural commune and the entire Russian society in their possibility of leaping over the Caudine Forks of capitalism. The author argued, "Marx and Engels's statements are only for the Russian rural communes. They have never said that the entire Russian society can enter socialism without going through capitalism."[13] This argument was not appropriate and is hereby revised and corrected.

1.3 To save the Russian commune, there must be a "Russian Revolution"

On March 1, 1861, Tsar Alexander II promulgated a decree to abolish serfdom. Per that decree, all serfs were declared free, and serf-cultivated land was to be distributed between the serfs and the aristocratic landlords. The aristocratic landlords received long-term treasury bonds from the government after their land was distributed to the peasants. In return, the peasants were required to pay the government redemption fees for 49 consecutive years. This reform was a major turning point in Russian history, greatly impacting Russian society and its rural communes.

After the above reform, Russian rural communes fell into a perilous situation. The state (the Tsar's government) resorted to all forces concentrated in its hands to oppress the commune, dramatically compromising the commune's economic conditions. The commune became the exploitee of businessmen, landlords, and loan sharks. Contention among varied interests sharpened within the commune, engendering all forces of fragmentation. The oppression by the state and the worsening bourgeois exploitation pushed the Russian commune to the brink of extinction. Marx and Engels believed that to enable the Russian rural commune to "leap over" the Caudine Forks of capitalism, the Russian rural commune must be saved first, and its free development restored. To accomplish this, there must be a "Russian Revolution."

In the first draft of *Reply to Vera Zasulich* dated in 1861, Marx said,

> To save the Russian commune, there must be a Russian Revolution ... If the revolution takes place in time, if it concentrates all its forces to ensure the unfettered rise of the rural commune, the latter will soon develop as a regenerating element of Russian society and an element of superiority over the countries enslaved by the capitalist regime.[14]

In their 1882 Preface to the second Russian edition of *Manifesto of the Communist Party*, Marx and Engels went straight to the question,

> can the Russian obshchina (rural community), though greatly undermined, yet a form of the primeval common ownership of land, pass directly to the

higher form of communist common ownership? Or on the contrary, must it first pass through the same process of dissolution as constitutes the historical evolution of the West?

Then they offered their well-considered and well-formulated answer: "If the Russian Revolution becomes the signal for a proletarian revolution in the West, so that both complement each other, the present Russian common ownership of land may serve as the starting point for a communist development."[15]

What type is the "Russian Revolution" to Marx and Engels? A clarification is in order here. To this question, many researchers in China either offer no serious consideration, or they consider it a nonessential question. Some even misunderstand the "Russian Revolution" as a proletarian socialist revolution. For example, the author of the book *Going Deep in History—A Study of Marx's Concept of History* wrote, "Marx did not deny Russia's possibility of a non-capitalist path, as predicated on the proletarian revolution."[16] Obviously, the author understands the "Russian Revolution" as a proletarian socialist revolution. As another example, the author of *The Guide to Modern Materialism* said:

> Marx pointed out that if Russia absorbs all the positive fruits of capitalism in the West, it may achieve its rebirth by leaping over the Caudine Forks of capitalism … They also believe that the Russian socialist revolution will serve as the pioneer for and work in concert with the Western European proletarian revolution.[17]

These authors clearly conclude that the "Russian Revolution" would be a proletarian socialist revolution, which would precede the proletarian revolution in Western Europe. The author of *The History of Marxism (four volumes)* thus wrote on this issue:

> Marx and Engels hope that Russia, a typical Eastern country with its own complete semi-Asiatic structure, would be the first to blaze a path different from the West, achieve its social transformation, overthrow capitalism, and become an Eastern model totally different from the West, socially economically, and politically. Russia will develop according to its own potentiality to serve as an innovative model for the Eastern society.[18]

Though implicit, this author's conclusion again is that the "Russian Revolution," preceding the West in "overthrowing capitalism," would be nothing but a proletarian socialist revolution. The author of *The History of Marxist Philosophy (eight volumes)* argued,

> From Marx's reply to *Vera Zasulich*, including the three drafts (actually four drafts, with the fourth basically the same as the final text), it is still not clear what type of revolution the "Russian Revolution" is. However, in January 1882, Marx and Engels, at the request of Pyotr Lavrov (Russian), wrote a

Preface to the second Russian edition of *Manifesto of the Communist Party*, in which they analyzed the changes of the Russian situation since the 1848– 1849 European Revolution and pointed out that Russia has turned from a reactionary fortress in Europe into an advanced team of the European revolutionary movement.

The author then concluded that Marx observed that the Russian commune "tends toward socialism" and that "the Great October Socialist Revolution in Russia has won in its unique way. Marx's conclusion that the Russian revolution would be a pioneer for the European revolution was confirmed."[19]

It is not correct to understand Marx and Engels' "Russian Revolution" as a proletarian socialist revolution. First, this understanding does not conform to the original intention of Marx and Engels, as will be explained later. Second, this understanding is illogical. The premise that the Russian rural commune can "leap over" the Caudine Forks of capitalism is that Russia was a pre-capitalist country not yet undergoing capitalist development. Since a socialist revolution can only take place in capitalist countries (or countries of considerable capitalistic development), there would be a paradox between the author's following two arguments: (1) the Russian rural commune is likely to "leap over" the Caudine Forks of the capitalist system; (2) the "leaping over" would be realized through a Russian socialist revolution, or even through "overthrowing capitalism." It is paradoxical because a socialist revolution is not a possibility in a society that's still pre-capitalistic. Third, Marx and Engels always believed that the proletarian socialist revolution would first take place and be victorious in developed capitalist countries such as Britain, France, Germany, and the United States. This view remained in their later years. The idea that the proletarian socialist revolution may first occur in one or more countries with a weak capitalism was proposed by Lenin in *On the Slogan for a United Europe* in 1915 and *The Military Programme of the Proletarian Revolution* in 1916. We cannot retrofit Lenin's words by 30 years into the mouths of Marx and Engels.

Some researchers in China believe that the "Russian Revolution" spoken of by Marx and Engels refers to the new-democratic revolution. For instance, the author of *The Road to Oriental Society* said,

> Marx believes that the nature of the Russian Revolution is not a socialist revolution (this was mentioned when Engels criticized Tkachev in 1875), nor is it the old-fashioned bourgeois revolution in Western Europe in the 17th–18th century. Instead it is a new form of bourgeois-democratic revolution aimed at the transition to socialism. Although Marx has not made any direct statements, but according to his understanding and analysis of the nature of the Russian Revolution, we can infer his thoughts on the nature of the Russian Revolution.[20]

The proper understanding then is that the "Russian Revolution" mentioned by Marx is neither a socialist revolution, nor an old-style bourgeois democratic revolution. But it is debatable whether it would be "a new form of bourgeois-democratic revolution aimed at the transition to socialism." According to the new-democracy theory of Lenin and Mao Zedong, the new-democratic revolution must be led by the proletariat and its political party. Nevertheless, Marx and Engels made their relevant remarks in the early 1880s when the Russian proletariat was not yet mature enough to lead the revolution, and the political party of the proletariat capable of leading this revolution had not formed (the first Marxist group in Russia—Emancipation of Labor—was established in September 1883, after which the Russian Social Democratic Party led by Lenin was established). First, Marx and Engels never claimed that the "Russian Revolution" in their reference would be a revolution led by the proletariat and its political party. In addition, we cannot find, in their understanding and analysis of the nature of "Russian Revolution," any indication that the "Russian Revolution" might be a new-democratic revolution either. Second, anyone who understands the history of the Russian Revolution and the world proletarian revolution would know that the proletarian party led by Lenin (the Social Democratic Party) led the Russian Revolution of 1905 and the February Revolution of 1917, both revolutions with a nature of the new democracy. We cannot retroactively put such historical occurrences backward to Marx and Engels' time in the early 1880s.

Then, to Marx and Engels, what exactly is the "Russian Revolution"? Engels offered a clear answer in his 1894 afterword to "On Social Relations in Russia." Engels first quoted a paragraph from Marx's 1877 "Letter to Editor of the Otecestvenniye Zapisky" on Russia's road to social development:

> Now, in what way was my critic able to apply this historical sketch (The account of primitive accumulation in *Capital*) to Russia? Only this: if Russia is tending to become a capitalist nation, on the model of the countries of Western Europe,—and in recent years it has gone to great pains to move in this direction—it will not succeed without having first transformed a large proportion of its peasants into proletarians; and after that, once it has been placed in the bosom of the capitalist system, it will be subjected to its pitiless laws, like other profane peoples. That is all.

After the above quote of Marx, Engels said:

> Thus wrote Marx in 1877. At that time there were two governments in Russia: the Tsar's and that of the secret executive committee (*ispolnitel'nyj komitet*) of the terrorist conspirators. The power of this secret second government grew daily. The fall of tsardom seemed imminent; a revolution in Russia was bound to deprive the entire forces of European reaction of its mainstay, its great reserve army, and thus give the political movement of the West a mighty new impulse and, what is more, infinitely more favourable conditions in which to operate. No wonder that Marx advises the Russians to be in less of a hurry to make the leap over into capitalism.

But,

> the Russian revolution did not come. Tsardom got the better of terrorism, which even managed to drive all the propertied, "law-abiding" classes back into its arms for the time being. And in the seventeen years which have elapsed since that letter was written both capitalism and the dissolution of the peasant commune have made tremendous headway in Russia.[21]

These comments by Engels tell us that due to changes in Russian social and revolutionary conditions from 1877 to 1894, the possibility for the Russian rural commune to "leap over" the Caudine Forks of capitalism has been greatly weakened and even disappeared. Engels' discussion clearly indicates that the "Russian Revolution" spoken of by Marx and himself is neither a proletarian socialist revolution nor a new-democratic revolution led by the proletarian party, but a revolution to overthrow the Tsar's autocratic system, led by the government of the secret executive committee of terrorist conspirators, that is, a revolution led by the Narodnik and partisans of Narodnaya Volya to overthrow the tsarist government.

It is easy to understand the relationship between the "Russian Revolution" and the "Western proletarian revolution" after clarifying the nature of the "Russian Revolution." The concrete meaning of the sentence "If the Russian Revolution becomes the signal for a proletarian revolution in the West, so that both complement each other," from the preface to the 1882 Russian edition of the *Manifesto of the Communist Party* by Marx and Engels in 1882, has been explained by Engels in his afterword to "On Social Relations in Russia" in 1894. Engels said:

> Whether enough of this commune has been saved so that, if the occasion arises, as Marx and I still hoped in 1882, it could become the point of departure for communist development in harmony with a sudden change of direction in Western Europe, I do not presume to say. But this much is certain: if a remnant of this commune is to be preserved, the first condition is the fall of tsarist despotism—revolution in Russia. This will not only tear the great mass of the nation, the peasants, away from the isolation of their villages, which comprise their "mir", their "world", and lead them out onto the great stage, where they will get to know the outside world and thus themselves, their own situation and the means of salvation from their present distress; it will also give the labour movement of the West fresh impetus and create new, better conditions in which to carry on the struggle, thus hastening the victory of the modern industrial proletariat, without which present-day Russia can never achieve a socialist transformation, whether proceeding from the commune or from capitalism.[22]

It means that, on the one hand, if the Narodnik and partisans of Narodnaya Volya succeed in a revolutionary overthrow of the tsarist government, this revolution will give the labor movement of the West fresh impetus, and create better conditions in which to carry on the struggle, thus hastening the victory of proletarian socialist revolution in Western Europe. Because tsarist despotism is the most powerful bastion and defense for all reactionary forces in Europe, and as long as there exists such a reactionary fortress near Western Europe, all revolutions will be suppressed. On the other hand, after the victory of the proletarian revolution in Western Europe, all the positive results obtained by Western European capitalism will be used to support the socialist transformation in Russia, and thus "the present Russian common ownership of land may serve as the starting point for a communist development."

Due to the great significance of the "Russian Revolution" not only to the Russian society itself, but also to the proletarian socialist revolution in Western Europe, Marx and Engels paid much attention to the situation of the "Russian Revolution" and earnestly hoped that this revolution would happen soon. They also discussed the significant impact and far-reaching implications of the "Russian Revolution." In "On Social Relations in Russia" Engels wrote with great pride:

> Russia undoubtedly is on the eve of a revolution ... Here all the conditions of a revolution are combined, of a revolution that, started by the upper classes of the capital, perhaps even by the government itself, must be rapidly carried further, beyond the first constitutional phase, by the peasants; of a revolution that will be of the greatest importance for the whole of Europe, if only because it will destroy at one blow the last, so far intact, reserve of the entire European reaction.[23]

In "To the Workingmen of Europe in 1877" written in February and March of 1878, Engels pointed out:

> But a Russian revolution means more than a mere change of government in Russia herself. It means the disappearance of a vast, though unwieldy, military power which, ever since the French Revolution, has formed the backbone of the united despotisms of Europe. It means the emancipation of Germany from Prussia, for Prussia has already been the creature of Russia, and has only existed by leaning upon her. It means the emancipation of Poland. It means the awakening of the smaller Slavonic nationalities of Eastern Europe from the Panslavist dreams fostered among them by the present Russian government. And it means the beginning of an active national life among the Russian people themselves, and along with it the springing up of a real working-class movement in Russia. Altogether, it means such a change in the whole situation of Europe as must be hailed with joy by the workingmen of every country as a giant step towards their common goal—the universal emancipation of Labor.[24]

This argument profoundly and concretely illustrates the significance of the revolution led by the Russian Narodnik and partisans of Narodnaya Volya in overthrowing the tsarist despotism. The victory of the Russian revolution means not only the beginning of an active national life among the Russian people themselves, and along with it the springing up of a real working-class movement in Russia, but also changes in the whole situation of Europe. It will inspire the proletarian revolution in Western Europe and promote the realization of the proletarian emancipation. This is why Marx and Engels focus on the revolution led by the Russian Narodnik and partisans of Narodnaya Volya to overthrow the tsarist despotism.

Notes

1   Jin Yan & Bian Wu (1996). *Rural Communities, Reform and Revolution – Village Community Tradition and the Road to Russian Modernization.* Beijing, China: Central Compilation Press, 7.

2   *Collected Works of Marx and Engels* (Vol. 33). (1973). Beijing, China: People's Publishing House, 577.

3   *An Anthology of Marx and Engels* (Vol. 3). (2009). Beijing, China: People's Publishing House, 574. Emphasis added.

4   *An Anthology of Marx and Engels* (Vol. 3). (2009). Beijing, China: People's Publishing House, 573. Emphasis added.

5   *An Anthology of Marx and Engels* (Vol. 3). (2009). Beijing, China: People's Publishing House, 586.

6   *An Anthology of Marx and Engels* (Vol. 3). (2009). Beijing, China: People's Publishing House, 574.

7   *An Anthology of Marx and Engels* (Vol. 3). (2009). Beijing, China: People's Publishing House, 576–577.

8   *An Anthology of Marx and Engels* (Vol. 3). (2009). Beijing, China: People's Publishing House, 571.

9   *An Anthology of Marx and Engels* (Vol. 3). (2009). Beijing, China: People's Publishing House, 572.

10 *An Anthology of Marx and Engels* (Vol. 3). (2009). Beijing, China: People's Publishing House, 575–576.

11 *An Anthology of Marx and Engels* (Vol. 3). (2009). Beijing, China: People's Publishing House, 579.

12 *An Anthology of Marx and Engels* (Vol. 3). (2009). Beijing, China: People's Publishing House, 574.

13 Zhao Jiaxiang (1985). *A Brief Introduction to Marxist Theory of Social Formations.* Beijing, China: Peking University Press, 150.

14 *An Anthology of Marx and Engels* (Vol. 3). (2009). Beijing, China: People's Publishing House, 582.

15 *An Anthology of Marx and Engels* (Vol. 2). (2009). Beijing, China: People's Publishing House, 8.

16 Chen Xianda (1987). *Going Deep in History—A Study of Marx's Concept of History.* Shanghai, China: Shanghai People's Publishing House, 406.

17 Chen Yanqing et al. (1996). *The Guide to Modern Materialism.* Tianjin, China: Nankai University Press, 321.

18 Zhuang Fulin (1996). *The History of Marxism* (Vol. 1). Beijing, China: People's Publishing House, 655.

19 Huang Nansen et al. (1996). *The History of Marxist Philosophy.* (Vol. 3). Beijing, China: Beijing Publishing House, 349–350.

20 Xie Lin (1992). *The Road to Oriental Society.* Beijing, China: China Social Sciences Press, 150.

21 *An Anthology of Marx and Engels* (Vol. 4). (2009). Beijing, China: People's Publishing House, 462–463.
22 *An Anthology of Marx and Engels* (Vol. 4). (2009). Beijing, China: People's Publishing House, 466–467.
23 *An Anthology of Marx and Engels* (Vol. 3). (2009). Beijing, China: People's Publishing House, 401.
24 *Collected Works of Marx and Engels* (Vol. 19). (1963). Beijing, China: People's Publishing House, 158.

2 Comparison of the early and the late Marxian thought

It is not easy to give the time divide between early and late Marxian thought. The division may depend on the issues involved. With regard to the possibility for the Russian rural commune to "leap over" the Caudine Forks of capitalism, the so-called late thought of Marx refer to those formed after his "Letter to Editor of the Otecestvenniye Zapisky." Those before that time are considered his early and middle-aged thought.

No mind is immutable. Neither is Marx's. The thoughts of a mind can change in different manners. One's later thoughts may reflect the logical continuation, deepening, and development of one's former thoughts, with consistency and the same origin in thoughts. One's later thoughts may differ from and even negate one's previous thoughts. Changes in Marx's thoughts seem to be of the first case, as evident in an impartial analysis. However, some are prone to dichotomize between an early and a late Marx or lean towards the idea of "three Marxes" (early, middle, and late). They tend to put Marx of different times in opposition or mutual negation. This chapter offers an analysis of such views.

2.1 Marx's two ideas about "world history"

Some scholars in China contend that the early Marx insisted that all countries and nations, regardless of their specific situations, were destined for capitalism, and that the late Marx, on the other hand, believed that some countries and nations could avoid capitalism by "leaping over" the Caudine Forks of capitalism. Therefore, these scholars conclude that the early and late Marx contradicted each other on this issue.

This opinion fails to grasp the essence of Marx's thoughts. Following their theories of historical materialism and scientific socialism in the mid-1840s, Marx and Engels formed two seemingly contradictory but essentially identical views about "world history." Accurate understanding of these two thoughts of Marx will facilitate the analysis of the logical evolution in Marxian thought.

One idea of Marx is that bourgeois capitalism, per its nature, would open up the world market and extend its tentacles to every corner of the globe, forcing all nations to adopt the capitalist mode of production. In *Manifesto of the Communist Party*, they argued:

The bourgeoisie has through its exploitation of the world market given a cosmopolitan character to production and consumption in every country ... The bourgeoisie, by the rapid improvement of all instruments of production, by the immensely facilitated means of communication, draws all, even the most barbarian, nations into civilisation. The cheap prices of its commodities are the heavy artillery with which it batters down all Chinese walls, with which it forces the barbarians' intensely obstinate hatred of foreigners to capitulate. It compels all nations, on pain of extinction, to adopt the bourgeois mode of production; it compels them to introduce what it calls civilisation into their midst, i.e., to become bourgeois themselves. In one word, it creates a world after its own image.[1]

In 1867, Marx pointed out in the preface to the first German edition of *Capital*:

Intrinsically, it is not a question of the higher or lower degree of development of the social antagonisms that result from the natural laws of capitalist production. It is a question of these laws themselves, of these tendencies working with iron necessity towards inevitable results. The country that is more developed industrially only shows, to the less developed, the image of its own future.[2]

These two quotations demonstrate that Marx believed the "iron necessity" of capitalism, in the then-historical context, to extend to pre-capitalist countries.

Why should less industrialized countries learn from well-industrialized countries? Because the former suffered dual miseries: Both their own pre-capitalistic and the newly introduced capitalistic modes of production. Marx illustrated this idea with his own country, Germany. He said,

In all other spheres, we, like all the rest of Continental Western Europe, suffer not only from the development of capitalist production, but also from the incompleteness of that development. Alongside the modern evils, a whole series of inherited evils oppress us, arising from the passive survival of antiquated modes of production, with their inevitable train of social and political anachronisms.

Marx believes that varied social formations are a natural historical process, in which the capitalistic phase cannot be leaped over. He added,

And even when a society has got upon the right track for the discovery of the natural laws of its movement ... it can neither clear by bold leaps, nor remove by legal enactments, the obstacles offered by the successive phases of its normal development [, although] it can shorten and lessen the birth-pangs.[3]

Then, does this mean Marx believed that all countries and nations, regardless of their individuality, must uniformly go through capitalism? Of course not. Because

Marx also believed that, while the bourgeois capitalism was victoriously march-
ing through the world, it was simultaneously conceiving the conditions for its own
demise. First, capitalism enabled a productivity beyond its own capacity. Marx
and Engels said:

> The productive forces at the disposal of society no longer tend to further the
> development of the conditions of bourgeois property; on the contrary, they
> have become too powerful for these conditions, by which they are fettered,
> and so soon as they overcome these fetters, they bring disorder into the whole
> of bourgeois society, endanger the existence of bourgeois property. The con-
> ditions of bourgeois society are too narrow to comprise the wealth created
> by them.[4]

Second, capitalism produced its own grave-digger—the proletariat. The bourgeoisie would create a world of its own design while the proletariat, a new communist world for mankind. As Marx and Engels stated:

> The advance of industry, whose involuntary promoter is the bourgeoisie,
> replaces the isolation of the labourers, due to competition, by their revolution-
> ary combination, due to association. The development of Modern Industry,
> therefore, cuts from under its feet the very foundation on which the bour-
> geoisie produces and appropriates products. What the bourgeoisie, therefore,
> produces, above all, are its own grave-diggers. Its fall and the victory of the
> proletariat are equally inevitable.[5]

The proletariat will establish "an association in which the free development of
each is the condition for the free development of all,"[6] namely, a new communist
society.

    Therefore, to Marx and Engels, the world proletarian revolution was not prem-
ised on all countries and nations adopting the capitalist mode of production, but
on "the concerted act of predominant peoples" taking control of the world market
and enormous productive forces "all at once" and "simultaneously,"[7] as they said
in *The German Ideology*. The ubiquitous communication caused by the bourgeois
capitalism would bring historic revolutions to developed capitalist countries such
as England, America, France, and Germany and those not yet capitalistic into a
new society, namely, communism. After reviewing the historical situations at that
time, we can clearly see that there were still many pre-capitalist countries and
nations when Marx and Engels proclaimed the foreseeable demise of capitalism,
a proclamation seen in their *Manifesto of the Communist Party* authored between
1847 and 1848 and in the words of *Capital*, "the knell of capitalist private property sounds."[8] If they indeed believed the proletarian revolution is premised on
all countries and nations embarking on capitalism, they should not have written
Manifesto of the Communist Party and *Capital* so early. They would instead per-
haps have elaborated how to enable pre-capitalist countries to embark on the path
of capitalist development.

After combining the two ideas (or more precisely, the two aspects of the same idea) of Marx and Engels, we conclude that Marx and Engels never considered it a premise of proletarian revolution that all countries and nations embark on capitalism. In reality, the early Marx and Engels have argued that some, even a considerable number of, countries and nations could "leap over" the Caudine Forks of capitalism. For instance, Marx and Engels pointed out in *The German Ideology*: "The competition with industrially more advanced countries, brought about by the expansion of international intercourse, is sufficient to produce a similar contradiction in countries with a backward industry." They further contended:

> Thus all collisions in history have their origin, according to our view, in the contradiction between the productive forces and the form of intercourse. Incidentally, to lead to collisions in a country, this contradiction need not necessarily have reached its extreme limit in this particular country ... The latent proletariat in Germany brought into view the competition of English industry.[9]

Engels also pointed out in the 19th issue of *The Principles of Communism*: The communist revolution in England, America, France, and Germany

> will have a powerful impact on the other countries of the world, and will radically alter the course of development which they have followed up to now, while greatly stepping up its pace. It is a universal revolution and will, accordingly, have a universal range.[10]

These arguments show that after history becomes "world history," because of ubiquitous international intercourse and the proletariat as a "world-historical existence," the history of pre-capitalist or industrially backward countries will be greatly altered so that they do not have to pass through "the Caudine Forks of capitalism" and instead will directly enter a new communist society. This is indeed the idea that pre-capitalist countries can "leap over" the Caudine Forks of capitalism. However, this idea at the time was still an abstract principle. In their later years, Marx and Engels crystallized it when discussing the Russian rural commune and Russia's future.

I would particularly point out that the early Marx and Engels already held that "the revolution in China" (the Taiping Rebellion) could become the "signal" of the Western revolution and "complement" it. In their 1853 article *Revolution in China and in Europe*, Marx and Engels raised the question: "Now, England having brought about the revolution of China, the question is how that revolution will in time react on England, and through England on Europe?" Marx believed "the revolution in China" would accelerate and exacerbate the industrial crisis in England. He said:

> The attention of our readers has often been called to the unparalleled growth of British manufactures since 1850. Amid the most surprising prosperity,

it has not been difficult to point out the clear symptoms of an approaching industrial crisis. Notwithstanding California and Australia, notwithstanding the immense and unprecedented emigration, there must ever, without any particular accident, in due time arrive a moment when the extension of the markets is unable to keep pace with the extension of British manufactures, and this disproportion must bring about a new crisis with the same certainty as it has done in the past. But, if one of the great markets suddenly becomes contracted, the arrival of the crisis is necessarily accelerated thereby. Now, the Chinese rebellion must, for the time being, have precisely this effect upon England.[11]

Marx further pointed out:

> Under these circumstances, as the greater part of the regular commercial circle has already been run through by British trade, it may safely be augured that the Chinese revolution will throw the spark into the overloaded mine of the present industrial system and cause the explosion of the long-prepared general crisis, which, spreading abroad, will be closely followed by political revolutions on the Continent. It would be a curious spectacle, that of China sending disorder into the Western World while the Western Powers, by English, French and American war-steamers, are conveying "order" to Shanghai, Nanking and the mouths of the Great Canal.[12]

These discussions indicate that Marx's thoughts on the relationship between revolutions in the East and in the West were consistent rather than contradictory throughout his life.

Let us return to the issue of "leaping over" the Caudine Forks of capitalism. As demonstrated by our historical and theoretical analysis above, Marx and Engels' proposition in their later years that the Russian rural commune and Russian society might "leap over" the Caudine Forks of capitalism is not a whim but the logical continuation, intensification, and development of their previous thoughts. Their subsequent thoughts crystallized and were thus congruent with their previous thoughts.

2.2 Prerequisites for Russian communes to "leap over the Caudine Forks"

Some in Chinese academia hold that Marx and Engels in their early years pinned their hope on the victory of the proletarian revolution in Western Europe, and in their later years felt "perplexed" about the "stagnation of the Western European revolution." They thus lost confidence in the Western European revolution and shifted their focus to the revolution in backward countries in the East, believing that the proletarian revolution in these countries would win initially and enter socialism before Western Europe.

This view is superficial and one-sided and fails to grasp the essence of Marx and Engels. In fact, two Marxian thoughts coexisted and played a concerted role.

On the one hand, he underestimated the lifespan of capitalism and mistook various drawbacks and conflicts, exposed in early capitalism due to its defects, as the sign of its demise, thus being optimistic about the proletarian victory in the Western Europe. Although he worked on summing up setbacks and failures of the Western European revolution, he always anchored his hope in its forthcoming victory. After 1848, the industry and commerce of England, France, and other countries in Europe prospered, in view of which Marx reviewed the failures of the 1848 Revolutions. He said,

> Given this general prosperity, wherein the productive forces of bourgeois society are developing as luxuriantly as it is possible for them to do within bourgeois relationships, a real revolution is out of the question. Such a revolution is possible only in periods when *both* of these *factors—the modern forces* of production and the *bourgeois forms of production*—come into *opposition* with each other.[13]

In *Preface to the Critique of Political Economy* written in 1859, Marx generalized the proletarian setbacks and failures mentioned above into an important principle of historical materialism that still furnishes great guidance for today's reality—the "two nevers" principle. He said:

> No social order is ever destroyed before all the productive forces for which it is sufficient have been developed, and new superior relations of production never replace older ones before the material conditions for their existence have matured within the framework of the old society.[14]

But Marx did not lose confidence in the proletarian revolution in Western Europe. He firmly believed that due to the contradictions inherent in capitalism, the economic crisis of capitalism is bound to erupt and trigger a new revolution. He said with pride: "*A new revolution is only a consequence of a new crisis. The one, however, is as sure to come as the other.*"[15] In his letter to Ferdinand Lassalle on February 22, 1858, when detailing his progress in writing *Capital*, he said:

> Now that I am at last ready to set to work after 15 years of study, I have an uncomfortable feeling that turbulent movements from without will probably interfere after all. Never mind. If I finish too late and thus find the world no longer attentive to such subjects, the fault is clearly my own.[16]

That is to say, Marx at that time believed that the storm of the world proletarian revolution was about to come. The capitalist system might have died out before the completion of *Capital*, and people would no longer be attentive to works that researched and criticized the capitalist system. Engels also had high hopes and optimism for the proletarian revolution in Western Europe. In the article *To the Working Men of Europe in 1877*, he said with joy:

Wherever we look in Europe, the working-class movement is progressing, not only favorably but rapidly, and what is more, everywhere in the same spirit. Complete harmony is restored, and with it constant and regular inter- course, in one way or another, between the workmen of the different coun- tries ... These men can now proudly exclaim: "The International has done its work; it has fully attained its grand aim—the union of the Proletariat of the whole world in the struggle against their oppressors."[17]

Marx, and especially Engels, in their later years realized that capitalism still had vitality with constant self-adjustment, and would not perish for the time being. Engels even publicly acknowledged that his hope for a victorious socialist revo- lution via a sweeping attack in 1848 and 1871 was "wrong" and "unfruitful," a kind of "fog" or "an illusion."[18] Due to historical limitations, however, Marx and Engels failed to foresee that even today, more than a hundred years after their deaths, capitalism has not yet shown signs of foreseeable extinction. Apparently, in their time, they did not lose hope for a proletarian victory in Western Europe.

In this case, why did Marx and Engels care so much about the revolution of the Russian Narodniks and Narodnaya Volya to overthrow the tsarist govern- ment, and why did they hope that it would win as soon as possible? Because Marx had another idea that capitalism would spread to pre-capitalist countries. Though decaying in Western Europe, capitalism would be new and vital when introduced beyond Western Europe. If this happened, even if the proletarian revolution in Western Europe won, this victory would inevitably be crushed in this little corner of the world by the newest capitalistic countries. Marx pointed out in a letter to Engels on October 8, 1858:

There is no denying that bourgeois society has for the second time experi- enced its 16th century, a 16th century which, I hope, will sound its death knell just as the first ushered it into the world. The proper task of bourgeois society is the creation of the world market, at least in outline, and of the production based on that market. Since the world is round, the colonisation of California and Australia and the opening up of China and Japan would seem to have completed this process. For us, the difficult question is this: on the Continent revolution is imminent and will, moreover, instantly assume a socialist character. Will it not necessarily be crushed in this little corner of the earth, since the movement of bourgeois society is still, in the ascendant over a far greater area?[19]

Marx insisted on this thought, based on which he advised the Russians in his later years "to be in less of a hurry to make the leap into capitalism"[20] and hoped that the Russian commune would "leap over" the Caudine Forks of capitalism for a direction transition into socialism.

Some say that Marx and Engels believed that the proletarian revolution would prevail first in the backward Eastern countries which would enter socialism before Western Europe. As I said before, this is a way of putting Lenin's thought into Marx and Engels' mouths. It is important to point out that Marx and Engels had never held that the proletarian revolution in the backward Eastern countries could occur and prevail earlier than in Western Europe. They actually sharply criticized this thought and repeatedly explained that the proletarian victory in Western Europe is a prerequisite for backward Eastern countries to forgo the torments of capitalism.

First of all, Marx and Engels believed that only after the proletarian victory in Western Europe could the backward Eastern countries acquire the material and technological foundations for a socialist transformation. These countries, however, were short of the above foundations at the time. Such foundations could only come from industrialized Western capitalist countries. Since socialism and capitalism are fundamentally opposed social systems, the Western ruling bourgeoisie would never hand over the material and technological foundations created by capitalist industrialization to the backward Eastern countries' socialist transformation and in so doing incur self-destruction. Therefore, only after Western Europe overthrew the bourgeois rule through the proletarian socialist revolution could the backward Eastern countries utilize all positive results created by the Western European capitalist system to carry out their own socialist transformation. Engels pointed out in a letter to the Russian Narodnik theorist Nikolai Danielson on February 24, 1893: "No doubt the commune and to a certain extent the artel, contained germs which under certain conditions might have developed and saved Russia the necessity of passing through the torments of the capitalistic regime." However,

> the first condition required to bring this about was *the impulse from without*, the change of economic system in the Occident of Europe, the destruction of the capitalist system in the countries where it had originated ... If we in the West had been quicker in our own economic development, if we had been able to upset the capitalistic regime some ten or twenty years ago, there might have been time yet for Russia to cut short the tendency of her own evolution towards capitalism.[21]

But unfortunately, during this period, the capitalist economies of the United Kingdom, France, the United States, Germany, and other countries made considerable progress, while the Russian commune faded away.

> We can only hope that the change to a better system, with us, may come soon enough to save, at least in some of the remoter portions of your country, institutions which may, under those circumstances, be called upon to fulfil a great future. But facts are facts, and we must not forget that these chances are getting less and less every year.[22]

In his afterword to "On Social Relations in Russia" (1894), Engels pointed out: "The victory of the West European proletariat over the bourgeoisie, and, linked to this, the replacement of capitalist production by socially managed production— that is the necessary precondition for raising the Russian commune to the same level." Without the proletarian victory in Western Europe, "present-day Russia can never achieve a socialist transformation, whether proceeding from the commune or from capitalism."[23] That is, in Engels' view, proceeding from the commune, Russia was unable to embark on the socialist path earlier than the Western developed capitalist countries. Even if Russia embarked on capitalism, due to its backward economy and culture, it would still be impossible for it to enter socialism earlier than Western developed capitalist countries.

Second, Engels believed that only when the proletarian victory in Western Europe became an example of socialist transformation for the backward Eastern countries could the latter follow this example in their own socialist transformation. Engels made this clear in the letter to Nikolai Danielson and in his afterword to "On Social Relations in Russia." He pointed out that if the backward countries need to leap over the harsh torments of the capitalist system,

> the example and the active assistance of the hitherto capitalist West is an indispensable condition for this. Only when the capitalist economy has been relegated to the history books in its homeland and in the countries where it flourished, only when the backward countries see from this example "how it's done", how the productive forces of modern industry are placed in the service of all as social property—only then can they tackle this shortened process of development.

Engels also emphasized that the sequence of this process is universal. He said: "And this is true of all countries in the pre-capitalist stage, not only Russia."[24] Engels offered noteworthy points here. First, Marx and Engels' idea on "leaping over" the capitalist torments had general applicability. This is to say, after the proletarian victory in the Western developed capitalist countries, all pre-capitalist countries may (or even necessarily) "leap over" the harsh torments of capitalism. Second, even if an economically and cultural backward country won the socialist victory and embarked on its socialist construction under certain historical conditions, its endeavor would be arduous due to the lack of a model from Western developed countries. Meanwhile, the undeveloped Eastern countries would have to endure more time, more frustrations, and even failures. This was fully manifested by the disintegration of the Soviet Union in late 20th century, the upheavals in Eastern Europe, the tortuous roads that China traveled before its reforms and opening-up, and its subsequent challenges.

Therefore, Marx and Engels' later idea that backward countries might "leap over" the torments of capitalism did not mean that they believed "the Western European revolution was deadlocked" or that they had lost confidence in the Western European revolution or felt "confused," disappointed, and frustrated, but that they firmly believed the Western European proletarian revolution would erupt and win in the near future. To Marx and Engels, without the proletarian victory in Western Europe, the backward countries are simply incapable of "leaping over" the capitalistic torments. To them, accepting the above "leaping over" capability was synonymous with believing the proletarian victory would occur first in

Western Europe. Thus, it is a serious misunderstanding of Marx and Engels to dichotomize between the proletarian victory in Western Europe and the backward Eastern countries' leaping over of capitalistic torments.

2.3 Comparison between Marx's early and late thought

Let's first examine Marx's thoughts on Russia's social development in his early years, and then analyze the similarities and differences between his early and late thought.

In his early years, Marx emphasized the common nature and path between the Russian commune and the Western European commune. He never or rarely addressed the particularities of the two. The public land ownership of the Russian commune, like in Western Europe, would inevitably transform into a land owner-ship to suit the capitalist mode of production. Marx offered many arguments on this issue, the most important of which are presented below to substantiate my views.

In a footnote to *Critique of Political Economy (Part I)* that Marx wrote in 1858–1859, he pointed out:

> At present an absurdly biased view is widely held, namely that *primitive* com-munal property is a specifically Slavonic, or even an exclusively Russian, phenomenon. It is an early form which can be found among Romans, Teutons and Celts, and of which a whole collection of diverse patterns (though some-times only remnants survive) is still in existence in India. A careful study of Asiatic, particularly Indian, forms of communal property would indicate that the disintegration of different forms of primitive communal ownership gives rise to diverse forms of property. For instance, various prototypes of Roman and Germanic private property can be traced back to certain forms of Indian communal property.[25]

In chapter 52 of *Capital Volume III*, Marx quoted from and concurred with the German economist F. List's book *Die Ackerverfassung, die Zwergwirtschaft und die Auswanderung*. Here is List's passage:

> The prevalence of a self-sufficient economy on large estates demonstrates solely the lack of civilisation, means of communication, domestic trades and wealthy cities. It is to be encountered, therefore, throughout Russia, Poland, Hungary and Mecklenburg. Formerly, it was also prevalent in England; with the advance of trades and commerce, however, this was replaced by the breaking up into middle estates and the leasing of land.

Marx cited List to show that all landed property would transform into a form befit-ting the capitalist mode of production. He said:

> We have seen that the continual tendency and law of development of the capitalist mode of production is more and more to divorce the means of

production from labour, and more and more to concentrate the scattered means of production into large groups, thereby transforming labour into wage-labour and the means of production into capital. And to this tendency, on the other hand, corresponds the independent separation of landed property from capital and labour or the transformation of all landed property into the form of landed property corresponding to the capitalist mode of production.[26]

In letters to Engels on February 10, 1870 and to Paul and Laura Lafargue on March 5, 1870, Marx spoke highly of *The Condition of the Working Class in Russia* written by Russian Narodnik theorist N Flerovsky. In the letter to Engels, Marx said:

> I have read the first 150 pages of *Flerovsky's* book (they are taken up by Siberia, North Russia and Astrakhan). This is the first work to tell the truth about Russian economic conditions. The man is a determined enemy of what he calls "Russian optimism". I never held very rosy views of this communistic Eldorado, but Flerovsky surpasses all expectations.[27]

Probably because Marx had not finished reading this book, he misunderstood Flerovsky's thoughts. As a Narodnik, Flerovsky held "optimistic" views of the Russian rural commune, rather than being "a determined enemy of 'Russian optimism'." When Marx wrote to Paul and Laura Lafargue, he had finished reading the book, fully understood Flerovsky, and corrected his previous misunderstanding. Marx said in this second letter:

> *The Condition of the Working Class in Russia* written by Flerovsky is an excellent work. I am very happy, now I can read it more smoothly by using dictionary. This book describes the entire economic situation of Russia for the first time. This is a very serious book. The author traveled the country in 15 years, from the western border to the eastern border of Siberia, from the White Sea to the Caspian Sea, the only purpose is to study the facts and expose the traditional lies. Of course, he still has some illusions about the infinite perfection of the Russian nation and the nature of the Russian-style commune ownership. But this is not the main thing. After studying his works, I am convinced that the magnificent Russian revolution is inevitable in Russia, and is approaching, of course, it has a primary form that is compatible with the current level of development in Russia.[28]

Here Marx severely criticized Flerovsky's view on the Russian rural commune, pointing out that "he has some illusions about the infinite perfection of the Russian nation and the nature of the Russian-style *commune ownership*."[29] In these two letters, Marx made clear his views on the future of the Russian rural communes: "I never held very rosy views of this communistic Eldorado." That is, before 1870, Marx rarely mentioned or held little illusion that the Russian commune might "leap over" the Caudine Forks of capitalism.

A comparison of Marx's early and late thoughts about the Russian commune and its development trajectory clearly indicates their commonalities and differences but no contradictions.

First, in his early years, Marx emphasized the universality of rural communes in history. In his later years, Marx emphasized the particularity of Russian rural communes: In Western Europe, rural communes and their land ownership dissolved because they hindered economic development, and by Marx's time, only "residues" remained.

> However, the situation of the Russian commune is absolutely different from that of the primitive communities in the West [Western Europe]. Russia is the only European country in which communal property has maintained itself on a vast, nationwide scale. But at the same time, Russia exists in a modern historical context: it is contemporaneous with a higher culture, and it is linked to a world market in which capitalist production is predominant.[30]

However, in his later years, Marx did not deny the universality of rural communes and their land ownership in history.

Second, in his early years, Marx emphasized the primitiveness, barbarism, and backwardness of Russian rural communes. In his later years, he emphasized that Russian rural communes may develop as "the fulcrum for social regeneration in Russia" and may "develop as the starting point of communist development." It may "develop as a regenerating element of Russian society and an element of superiority over the countries enslaved by the capitalist regime."[31] However, in his later years, Marx did not deny the primitiveness, barbarism, and backwardness of the Russian rural communes, but, like in his early years, he did not hold rosy views on the Russian rural communes. He actually elaborated the primitiveness, barbarism, and backwardness of the Russian rural communes as they were. In the first draft of *Marx's Correspondence to Zasulich*, he pointed out:

> One debilitating feature of the "agricultural commune" in Russia is inimical to it in every way. This is its isolation, the lack of connection between the lives of different communes. It is not an immanent or universal characteristic of this type that the commune should appear as a *localised microcosm*. But wherever it does so appear, it leads to the formation of a more or less central despotism above the communes.[32]

In the second draft, the same thought was repeated.[33] In the third draft, this thought was deepened and crystallized:

> But what of the anathema which strikes the commune – its isolation, the lack of connection between the lives of different communes, that *localised microcosm* which has so far denied it all historical initiative? It would vanish in the general upheaval of Russian society … In order to [secure the same economic benefits] equalise the chances for labour, they therefore divided

the land into a number of areas according to natural and economic varia-
tions, and then subdivided these areas into as many plots as there were till-
ers. Finally, everyone received a patch of land in each area. It goes without
saying that this arrangement, perpetuated by the Russian commune to this
day, cuts across agronomic requirements [whether farming is on a collective
or a private, individual basis]. Apart from other disadvantages, it compels a
dispersion of strength and time.[34]

Third, in his early years, Marx emphasized the historical inevitability of the disintegration of rural communes in China and its progressive role in social development. In his later years, Marx emphasized that rural communes might not
disintegrate in the then-historical environment to herald communism after the
proletarian victory in Western Europe. However, he did not deny the inevitable
disintegration of Russian rural communes, and affirmed that they were endan-
gered by internal fragmentations and external corrosions. Marx pointed out in the
first draft of *Marx–Zasulich Correspondence*: The communes'

> dualism may eventually become a source of disintegration. Apart from the
> influence of a hostile environment, the mere accumulation over time of
> movable property, beginning with wealth in livestock and even extending
> to wealth in serfs, combines with the ever more prominent role played by
> movables in agriculture itself and with a host of other circumstances, insepa-
> rable from such accumulation, which would take me too far from the central
> theme. All these factors, then, serve to dissolve economic and social equality,
> generating within the commune itself a conflict of interests which leads, first,
> to the conversion of arable land into private property, and ultimately to the
> private appropriation of forests, pastures, waste ground, etc.

Then, Marx pointed out the various destructive forces from outside the commune.
He said:

> After the so-called emancipation of the peasantry, the state placed the
> Russian commune in abnormal economic conditions; and since that time, it
> has never ceased to weigh it down with the social force concentrated in its
> hands. Exhausted by tax demands, the commune became a kind of inert mat-
> ter easily exploited by traders, landowners and usurers. This oppression from
> without unleashed the conflict of interests already present at the heart of the
> commune, rapidly developing the seeds of its disintegration. But that is not
> all. [At the peasant's expense, it grew as in a hothouse those excrescences of
> the capitalist system that can be most easily acclimatised (the stock exchange,
> speculation, banks, share companies, railways), writing off their deficits,
> advancing profits to their entrepreneurs, etc., etc.] At the peasant's expense,
> the state [lent a hand to] grew in hothouse conditions certain branches of the
> Western capitalist system which, in no way developing the productive prem-
> ises of agriculture, are the best suited to facilitate and precipitate the theft of

its fruits by un productive middlemen. In this way, it helped to enrich a new capitalist vermin which is sucking the already depleted blood of the "rural commune."

Marx concluded: "Unless it is broken by a powerful reaction, this combination of destructive influences must naturally lead to the death of the rural commune."[35]

By now, we have seen that, between his early and late years, Marx did not fundamentally change in his views about social history or the rural communes.

Notes

1   *An Anthology of Marx and Engels* (Vol. 2). (2009). Beijing, China: People's Publishing House, 35, 35–36.
2   *An Anthology of Marx and Engels* (Vol. 5). (2009). Beijing, China: People's Publishing House, 8.
3   *An Anthology of Marx and Engels* (Vol. 5). (2009). Beijing, China: People's Publishing House, 9, 9–10.
4   *An Anthology of Marx and Engels* (Vol. 2). (2009). Beijing, China: People's Publishing House, 37.
5   *An Anthology of Marx and Engels* (Vol. 2). (2009). Beijing, China: People's Publishing House, 43.
6   *An Anthology of Marx and Engels* (Vol. 2). (2009). Beijing, China: People's Publishing House, 53.
7   *An Anthology of Marx and Engels* (Vol. 1). (2009). Beijing, China: People's Publishing House, 538–539.
8   *An Anthology of Marx and Engels* (Vol. 5). (2009). Beijing, China: People's Publishing House, 874.
9   *An Anthology of Marx and Engels* (Vol. 1). (2009). Beijing, China: People's Publishing House, 567, 567–568.
10 *An Anthology of Marx and Engels* (Vol. 1). (2009). Beijing, China: People's Publishing House, 687.
11 *An Anthology of Marx and Engels* (Vol. 2). (2009). Beijing, China: People's Publishing House, 609, 610.
12 *An Anthology of Marx and Engels* (Vol. 2). (2009). Beijing, China: People's Publishing House, 612.
13 *An Anthology of Marx and Engels* (Vol. 2). (2009). Beijing, China: People's Publishing House, 176. Emphasis added.
14 *An Anthology of Marx and Engels* (Vol. 2). (2009). Beijing, China: People's Publishing House, 592.
15 *An Anthology of Marx and Engels* (Vol. 2). (2009). Beijing, China: People's Publishing House, 176. Emphasis added.
16 *An Anthology of Marx and Engels* (Vol. 10). (2009). Beijing, China: People's Publishing House, 150.
17 *Collected Works of Marx and Engels* (Vol. 19). (1963). Beijing, China: People's Publishing House, 149.
18 *An Anthology of Marx and Engels* (Vol. 4). (2009). Beijing, China: People's Publishing House, 538–542.
19 *An Anthology of Marx and Engels* (Vol. 10). (2009). Beijing, China: People's Publishing House, 166.
20 *An Anthology of Marx and Engels* (Vol. 4). (2009). Beijing, China: People's Publishing House, 463.

21 Emphasis added.
22 *An Anthology of Marx and Engels* (Vol. 10). (2009). Beijing, China: People's Publishing House, 649, 650.
23 *An Anthology of Marx and Engels* (Vol. 4). (2009). Beijing, China: People's Publishing House, 457, 466–467.
24 *An Anthology of Marx and Engels* (Vol. 4). (2009). Beijing, China: People's Publishing House, 459.
25 *Collected Works of Marx and Engels* (Vol. 31). (1998). Beijing, China: People's Publishing House, 426. Emphasis added.
26 *An Anthology of Marx and Engels* (Vol. 7). (2009). Beijing, China: People's Publishing House, 1001–1002.
27 *Collected Works of Marx and Engels* (Vol. 32). (1975). Beijing, China: People's Publishing House, 421. Emphasis added.
28 *An Anthology of Marx and Engels* (Vol. 10). (2009). Beijing, China: People's Publishing House, 325.
29 Emphasis added.
30 *Collected Works of Marx and Engels* (Vol. 19). (1963). Beijing, China: People's Publishing House, 444.
31 *Collected Works of Marx and Engels* (Vol. 19). (1963). Beijing, China: People's Publishing House, 269, 326, 441.
32 *An Anthology of Marx and Engels* (Vol. 3). (2009). Beijing, China: People's Publishing House, 575. Emphasis added.
33 *Collected Works of Marx and Engels* (Vol. 19). (1963). Beijing, China: People's Publishing House, 445.
34 *An Anthology of Marx and Engels* (Vol. 3). (2009). Beijing, China: People's Publishing House, 587, 587–588. Emphasis added.
35 *An Anthology of Marx and Engels* (Vol. 3). (2009). Beijing, China: People's Publishing House, 574, 476–577, 577.

3 Difference and consistency between Engels' and Marx's thoughts

There are scholars in both China and abroad who believe that contradiction exists not only between Marx's early and late views on the Russian rural commune but between Marx's and Engels' views on the same issue. This is a misunderstanding. I believe that their views on the issue are essentially consistent. There may be differences but no contradictions.

3.1 Engels' criticism of the Russian Narodniks' mistakes

Russian populism (the Narodniks) was a utopian agricultural socialist idea that represented the interests of small producers. It was born in Russia in the 1860s and 1870s. Narodniks considered themselves the "essence" of the people and proposed to "go among the people" to mobilize the overthrow of the Tsar's autocracy. They regarded capitalism in Russia as a fortuity unlikely to occur and denied the proletariat as the most advanced and revolutionary class. They regarded the Russian rural commune as the embryo and foundation of socialism and the peasants as the main revolutionary force, emphasized the so-called special path of Russian development, hoped to curb capitalism in Russia, and advocated the establishment of a socialist system based on rural communes. Considering the development of world history and Russia's situation at that time, and based on historical materialism, Engels sharply criticized these misconceived ideas of Russian populists.

3.1.1 Engels' criticism of Russian Narodniks' utopian agricultural socialism

As early as the 1840s, when Marx and Engels set up the scientific socialism, worship of the magical power of rural communes began to surge among Russian intellectuals. The Narodniks were disciples of this worship. They believed socialism would materialize in Russia faster and more easily than in Western Europe. Their main reasons were: (1) Neither the urban proletariat nor the urban bourgeoisie existed in Russia, and the peasant only needed to fight against the political power of an authoritarian government. This struggle could easily be won. (2) The combination of labor and the rural system was a social feature unlike and superior to Western Europe. The village community would become "the cornerstone of the future society that we all dream of."[1] (3) Russian peasants, "as born communists and the chosen people of socialism,"[2] "are infinitely closer to socialism than the poor, god-forsaken West European proletarians."[3] Engels made trenchant criticism of these mistaken views.

Regarding Narodniks' first reason, Engels retorted that the transformation sought by modern socialism was a process in which the proletariat defeated the bourgeoisie, destroyed class, and established a new society without class and class differences. The barbarians and semi-barbarians of the primitive era had no class and class differences, and each nation had experienced this condition. We were by no means going to restore this state because class differences would inevitably emerge due to the development of productivity. Only when productivity reached a certain level, a level deemed high even against current conditions, could the elimination of class differences become true progress, progress sustainable with no further stagnation and regression in productivity. Only in the hands of the bourgeoisie may productivity reach such a high level. Therefore, the bourgeoisie, like the proletariat, was also a prerequisite for the socialist revolution.

> Hence a man who says that this revolution can be more easily carried out in a country where, although there is no proletariat, there is no bourgeoisie either, only proves that he has still to learn the ABC of socialism.[4]

This thought of Engels has important practical significance. It tells us that only when social productivity develops to a high degree can we eliminate all class and class differences. Eliminating class and class differences factitiously under low productivity is not "real progress," as it cannot "be sustained" and will cause stagnation and regression in the production mode of society. This truth has been demonstrated by the reality of some countries.

For the second reason of the Narodniks, Engels believed that the Russian rural commune was not a magical thing, but a clan social system before the civilized era and primitive agricultural communism. The public ownership of rural communes was a land ownership prevalent in the Indo-European people in the primitive era. It was still operative in India and even partially so in Germany at the time, only eliminated forcibly in Ireland and Scotland lately. Therefore, the commune system was not peculiar to Russia. It was a form of ownership that had already declined. Historically, it had been a phenomenon common to all nations. Of course, Engels also noticed that Russia was indeed the only country that had preserved the commune system nationwide, but that was not evidence for Russia's superiority over Western European society. In Western Europe, developed productivity and expanded social interaction had gradually dissolved its original communal land ownership, which increasingly became a shackle on agricultural production. Russia's retention of the commune system could only show that the country's agricultural production and its corresponding rural social relations were still undeveloped. The prevalence of Russian rural communes was a sign of the general backwardness of Russian society, far behind the level of modern civilization.

For the third reason of the Narodniks, Engels believed that the insular backwardness of the Russian commune was manifested particularly in the mode and
scope of its members' activities. Russian peasants only lived and labored in their
own communes. The rest of the world did not exist for them until it began to
interfere with their commune affairs. To them, the whole world was the "general
commune assembly." Such isolation of the communes led to similar but rarely
concerted interests across the country, furnishing the basis for the Eastern autocracy. Such commune members were not so much pioneer voters of socialism as
primitive members surviving on subsistence. The claim that they were closer to
socialism than the Western European proletariat was largely sheer nonsense.[5]

In the afterword to "On Social Relations in Russia," Engels said: The primary
factor for socialist transformation of the Russian rural commune "cannot come
from the commune itself"; "at no time or place has the agrarian communism that
arose out of gentile society developed anything of its own accord but its own
disintegration"; "The Russian commune has existed for hundreds of years without ever providing the impetus for the development of a higher form of common
ownership out of itself."[6] On this basis, Engels discussed a fundamental principle
of historical materialism, which is still guiding China's reforms and interactions
with the world. Engels continued:

> It is an historical impossibility that a lower stage of economic development
> should solve the enigmas and conflicts which did not arise, and could not
> arise, until a far higher stage. All forms of gentile community which arose
> before commodity production and individual exchange have one thing in
> common with the future socialist society: that certain things, means of pro-
> duction, are subject to the common ownership and the common use of certain
> groups. This one shared feature does not, however, enable the lower form of
> society to engender out of itself the future socialist society, this final and most
> intrinsic product of capitalism. Any given economic formation has its own
> problems to solve, problems arising out of themselves; to seek to solve those
> of another, utterly alien formation would be absolutely absurd.[7]

In the preface to *A Contribution to the Critique of Political Economy* written in
1859, Marx said:

> No social order is ever destroyed before all the productive forces for which
> it is sufficient have been developed, and new superior relations of production
> never replace older ones before the material conditions for their existence
> have matured within the framework of the old society. Mankind thus inevita-
> bly sets itself only such tasks as it is able to solve, since closer examination
> will always show that the problem itself arises only when the material condi-
> tions for its solution are already present or at least in the course of formation.[8]

A comparison of Engels' and Marx's arguments clearly indicates that Engels not
only adhered to but deepened and consolidated Marx's basic ideas. Engels also

illuminated the practical guidance embedded in Marx's ideas. Engels said: "And this applies to the Russian commune no less than to the South Slav zádruga, the Indian gentile economy or any other savage or barbaric form of society characterised by the common ownership of the means of production."[9] The practical significance of Marx and Engels' thought is that the development of a social form is a natural historical process. Do not overemphasize the "transcendent power" of a social stage and the so-called "leap-forward" out of historical context. Though precipitous, a "leap-forward" may engender enduring adverse consequences. It may be helpful for our hot-headed and over-optimistic comrades of the "leaping-forward" ideology to read what Marx said in the preface to the first edition of *Capital Volume I,*

> My standpoint is that the evolution of the economic formation of society is viewed as a process of natural history ... And even when a society has got upon the right track for the discovery of the natural laws of its movement—and it is the ultimate aim of this work, to lay bare the economic law of motion of modern society—it can neither clear by bold leaps, nor remove by legal enactments, the obstacles offered by the successive phases of its normal development.[10]

We also want to remind those hot-headed comrades to review the history of China's socialist construction and not to repeat its mistake of the "Great Leap Forward" in 1958.

3.1.2 *Engels' criticism of the Russian Narodniks' mistake in denying the historical inevitability and progressiveness of Russia's development of capitalism*

In the late 1880s and early 1890s, due to changes in the world and in Russia's own situation, Engels saw no possibility for the Russian rural commune to "leap over" the Caudine Forks of capitalism. The only way for revolution to happen would be through capitalistic development. Although Russia's path to capitalistic development would bring along its own torments, it was inevitable in the course of historical progress. Nikolai Danielson, a Russian populist ideologist, opposed Russia's development of capitalism and advocated large modern industry based on the Russian commune on the grounds that Russia's path to capitalism would bring suffering to workers, peasants, and the entire Russian society. Engels criticized this misconception mainly from the following two aspects.

First, Engels criticized Danielson's incorrect denial of the historical inevitability of capitalism in Russia. Engels argued that it was Danielson's wrong historical idealism that caused him to ignore the objective inevitability and historical context of social progress, which cannot be assessed by personal inclinations. As Engels pointed out, capitalistic development in Russia was an undeniable truth. "Our personal inclinations are an irrelevant matter, in spite of which, objective facts will stay and continue. The freer we are from personal inclinations, the more capable we are to assess facts as they are and will be." Hereby, Engels provided us an objective measure of history. Danielson saw the tremendous changes in Russia since its 1861 reforms in serfdom. Yet he denied the changes due to his personal dislike of them. Engels, however, believed that these changes were historically inevitable and represented social progress. He said,

> Since 1861, Russia began to develop its industry on a scale commensurate with its national size. People have long come to realize that, without industrialization powered by the steam engine, no nation will fully (or even largely) meet its need for industrial commodities. Consequently, that nation will not achieve eminence among the civilized nations. Russia has begun to mobilize itself, based on this realization, with arduous efforts.[11]

Second, Engels criticized Danielson's incorrect denial of capitalistic development in Russia on the pretext that improper policies of the Russian government had destroyed household and sideline industries in Russia. To Danielson, capitalistic development and its concomitant misery among the people could be attributed to the Russian government's incorrect policy on protective tariffs. To Engels, however, capitalistic development in Russia was an economic inevitability and had nothing to do with governmental policies. Engels believed that large machinery industry would inevitably drive out cottage and sideline industries on which the peasants sustained their survival. Such inevitable consequences were seen not only in Russia but also historically in the United Kingdom and Germany. The discussion of capitalistic development in Russia should focus not on whether it will drive out household manufacture and related agricultural enterprises, but on exploring how large-scale industrialization may develop in Russia. Engels said,

> The Russians had to decide whether *their own* grande industrie was to destroy their domestic manufacture, or whether the *import of English goods* was to accomplish this. *With* protection, the *Russians* effected it, *without* protection, the *English*. That seems to me perfectly evident.[12]

Engels also sharply criticized Danielson based on the relation between the foundation of the economy and the superstructure of society. Engels believed that the superstructure may only stimulate or stymie but never determine the general trajectory of the economic development. He said,

> All governments, be they ever so absolute, are *en dernier lieu* but the executors of the economic necessities of the national situation … they may accelerate or retard the economic development and its political and juridical consequences, but in the long run they must follow it. Whether the means by which the industrial revolution has been carried out in Russia have been the best for the purpose, is a question by itself which it would lead too far to discuss. For my purpose it is sufficient if I can prove that this industrial revolution, in itself, was unavoidable.[13]

Here, Engels offers us this inspiration: During China's reforms and its open contacts with the world, the proposition of any major policy must be based on whether it falls in line with the objective development of history, whether it enhances productivity, whether it enlarges our national power, and whether it betters its citizens' life. It should not be assessed on the basis of our phobia against capitalism or on the basis of the metaphysical debate between socialism and capitalism.

3.1.3 Engels' criticism of Russian populists' mistake in denying that historical progress comes at a price

Historical progress and its price are twin brothers in that historical progress must come at a price, while this price would be made up for with the progress of history. Danielson argued that developing capitalist large industry in Russia would lead to unemployment of workers, bankruptcy of farmers, food reduction, industrial products reduction, trade decline, price rises, and a wider gap between the rich and the poor, causing unbearable sufferings to its people. He said,

> Capitalistic development is engendering a revolution hitherto unseen anywhere. Its further development will lead to the bankruptcy (as already happening) and starvation of all the working people … The replacement by new large landowners of the peasants will produce millions of laborers without their own means of production and in turn destroy the domestic industrial market and cause the starvation of millions.

As Engels pointed out, the fundamental mistake of Danielson lay in his denial of the truth that historical progress comes at a price, which will be made up for with the progress of history. Engels said,

> [I]f Russia required after the Crimean War a grande industrie of her own, she could have it in one form only: the *capitalistic form*. And along with that form, she was obliged to take over all the consequences which accompany capitalistic grande industrie in all other countries.

This was particularly serious in the case of Russia, because

> Russia being *the last country seized upon* by the capitalist grande industrie, and at the same time the country *with by far the largest peasant population*, are such as must render the bouleversement caused by this economic change more acute than it has been anywhere else. The process of replacing some 500,000 pomeshchiki (landowners) and some eighty million peasants by a new class of *bourgeois* landed proprietors cannot be carried out but under fearful sufferings and convulsions. But history is about the most cruel of all goddesses, and she leads her triumphal car over heaps of corpses, not only in war, but also in "peaceful" economic development. And we men and women are unfortunately so stupid that we never can pluck up courage

to a real progress unless urged to it by sufferings that seem almost out of proportion.[14]

Engels also said,

> During the transition from the primitive agricultural community to capitalistic industrialization, it'd be impossible not to see tumultuous changes, including the disappearance of whole classes or their complete transformation into another. This will inevitably lead to grotesque pain and unmeasurable waste to life and productivity, as already seen in West Europe.

However, "capitalism is demonstrating a new prospect and hope ... No historical calamity occurs without its concomitant compensation." In history, "all things come to serve at human progress ... one way or another, along a tortuous journey ... The current economic reforms [in Russia] will be no exception."[15] Engels' idea carries the realistic implication that to judge whether our reforms and opening-up to the world are successful, or whether our strategies and policies are correct, we cannot only see the costs of the endeavor but also the fruits derived therefrom. The doubts cast upon our reforms due to attention paid only to the costs are incompatible with Engels' arguments.

3.1.4 Engels' criticism of Russian populists' "Grafting Theory"— "grafting" Russian rural communes with modern large industry to develop rural communes into socialism

Danielson, the Russian populist theorist, did not deny the backwardness of Russian rural communes, nor did he deny the necessity of developing modern large industry. What he opposed was developing capitalist large industry. He advocated "grafting" Western large industry upon Russian rural communes to develop the latter into socialism. Engels made an unsparing criticism of this "Grafting Theory."

First, to Engels, the Russian commune, as the receiver of the "graft," was a primitive, spontaneous, and isolated insularity. It was not based on socialized organized mass production and was very much removed from the *grande industrie*. With no capacity to incorporate or run modern *grande industrie*, the Russian commune would be shattered by the former once in contact with it. Therefore, it was utopian to make the rural commune a recipient of grafted modern *grande industrie*. In his letter to Danielson on February 24, 1893, Engels questioned,

> [I]n, or about, 1854 Russia started with the commune on the one hand, and the necessity of the grande industrie on the other. Now, if you take the whole state of your country into account, as it was at that date, do you see any possibility of the grande industrie being grafted on the peasants' commune in a form which would, on the one hand, make the development of that grande industrie possible, and on the other hand raise the primitive commune to the

rank of a social institution superior to anything the world has yet seen? And that while the whole Occident was still living under the capitalist regime? It strikes me that such an evolution, which would have surpassed anything known in history required other economic, political and intellectual conditions than were present at that time in Russia.[16]

Engels made a more thorough criticism of the "Grafting Theory" in his afterword to "On Social Relations in Russia,"

> But the mere fact that alongside the Russian peasant commune capitalist production in Western Europe is simultaneously approaching the point where it breaks down and where it points itself to a new form of production in which the means of production are employed in a planned manner as social property—this mere fact cannot endow the Russian commune with the power to develop this new form of society out of itself. How could it appropriate the colossal productive forces of capitalist society as social property and a social tool even before capitalist society itself has accomplished this revolution; how could the Russian commune show the world how to run large-scale industry for the common benefit, when it has already forgotten how to till its land for the common benefit?[17]

Second, as was the case in Russia, although a number of Russians were aware of the Western capitalist economy, the modern large industry, and the capitalistic predicament and the way out of it, few of these people resided within Russia. The Russian society largely consisted of two groups: The mass of Russian farmers and the "new pillars" of Russian society who admired capitalism. The former long resided in the insularity of their rural commune, undertaking extremely simple and menial work without knowing what modern large industry was at all, let alone how to manage it based on the principle of private ownership. The latter group of capitalism admirers tried all they could to lead Russia onto a capitalistic path. But for them, due to the lack of a recipient or base onto which to graft capitalism, the grafting was simply a delusion.

Third, the modern large industry to be grafted, nonexistent in Russia, came from the capitalist countries in Western Europe. Due to its incompatibility with socialism, capitalism would be digging its own grave if it allowed itself to be grafted upon the Russian commune to propel the latter into socialism in a world still dominated by capitalism. Western European capitalism would commit no such stupidity. In a capitalism-dominant world, socialism through grafting of capitalistic industry was simply paradoxical and unrealistic.

3.2 Differences between Engels' and Marx's thoughts

Views diverge on the interrelations between Engels and Marx concerning Russia's development. Some scholars emphasize the differences and even contradictions between Marx and Engels, while others, the consistency and even identity between the two. Both views are biased. I contend that between Marx and Engels, there are both differences and intrinsic consistency on this issue. Their differences are complementary rather than contradictory. Only an organic synthesis of both—neither differentiation nor identification between the two—will give full knowledge of Russia's development trajectory.

Four major differences exist between Engels and Marx on Russia's development.

First, after Marx passed away, owing to the further disintegration of Russian rural community, capitalism gained increasingly rapid development in Russia, making it a capitalist country. Therefore, Engels underscored, more prominently than Marx, the inevitability of the disintegration of Russian rural community. In his afterword to "On Social Relations in Russia," after quoting from the preface to the *Communist Manifesto* (second edition in Russian), a work he co-authored with Marx, Engels said,

> It should not be forgotten, however, that the considerable disintegration of Russian common property mentioned above has since advanced significantly. The defeats of the Crimean War had exposed Russia's need for rapid industrial development. Above all railways were needed, and these are not possible on a broad footing without large-scale domestic industry. The precondition for this was the so-called emancipation of the serfs; it marked the beginning of the capitalist era in Russia; but hence also the era of the rapid destruction of the common ownership of land. The redemption payments imposed on the peasants, together with increased taxes and the simultaneous reduction and deterioration of the land allotted to them, inevitably forced them into the hands of usurers, chiefly members of the peasant commune who had grown rich ... The traditional conditions of employment were thrown into confusion; there followed the breakdown which everywhere accompanies the transition from a subsistence economy to a "money economy" within the commune; large differences in wealth appeared between the members—debt turned the poorer into the slaves of the rich.

Under this condition, no "power in the world will be able to restore the Russian commune once its breakdown has reached a certain point."[18]

Second, when Marx was alive, the revolution in Russia was gathering momentum, through which the possibility of the outbreak of a proletarian revolution in Western Europe was huge. Therefore, he emphasized the need to save the Russian commune from all the extreme disasters brought about by the capitalist regime. After the death of Marx, the struggle of the Narodniks and the Narodnaya Volya to overthrow the tsarist government failed. Following this, Russia quickly embarked on capitalist development. Therefore, Engels emphasized the historical inevitability of Russia's embarking on capitalism. He said in the afterword of "On Social Relations in Russia": "When the old tsarist despotism continued unchanged after the defeats of the Crimean War and the suicide of Tsar Nicholas, only one road was open: the swiftest transition possible to capitalist industry."

The railways and factories were accompanied by the expansion of existing banks and the establishment of new ones; the emancipation of the peasants from serfdom instituted freedom of movement, in anticipation of the ensuing automatic emancipation of a large proportion of these peasants from land-ownership too. Thus in a short while all the foundations of the capitalist mode of production were laid in Russia. But the axe had also been taken to the root of the Russian peasant commune.

"And so the transformation of the country into a capitalist industrial nation, the proletarianisation of a large proportion of the peasantry and the decay of the old communistic commune proceeds at an ever quickening pace." Based on its economic prosperity, capitalism also matured politically. "In these circumstances the fledgling Russian bourgeoisie has the state completely in its power. In all economic matters of importance the state must do its bidding."[19]

Third, Marx emphasized that the artel of peasants in the Russian village commune helped the transition from the small-scale land economy to the cooperative economy. Engels emphasized the backwardness of the artel based on its emergence, characteristics, forms, and historical destiny. Engels believed that the artel in Russia was a very simple cooperative. He said:

> The artel in Russia is a widespread form of association, the simplest form of free co-operation, such as is found for hunting among hunting tribes. Word and content are not of Slavic but of Tatar origin ... That is why the artel developed originally in the North and East, by contact with Finns and Tatars, and not in the South-West.[20]

In addition, Engels believed that the artel in Russia was very primitive. One big characteristic of the artel is the collective responsibility of its members for one another to third parties—originally based on kinship—like the mutual liability and blood vengeance among the ancient Germans. In addition, Engels believed that the artel in Russia was a spontaneously established co-operative society that remained much undeveloped. Its predominance in Russia proved Russians' strong spirit of community, which alone however could not advance them from the artel to communism. Engels said:

> For that, it is necessary above all that the artel itself should be capable of development, that it shed its primitive form, in which, as we saw, it serves the workers less than it does capital, and rise *at least* to the level of the West European co-operative societies.[21]

Finally, Engels believed that the artel in Russia wasn't fit for the development of modern big industry; the cooperative commune in West Europe had proved itself capable of independent and mass industry; the Russian artel, however, possessed no such capability, and would, without further development, inevitably die upon contact with large modern industrialization.

Fourth, Engels' criticism of the Russian Narodniks was explicit and acute, as seen in his above-cited quotations. Marx's criticism of the Russian Narodniks was more implicit and mild. Why? Because the Russian Narodniks showeda particular interest in Marx's doctrines and activities. Marx used to have close contacts with some of them. Russian Narodnik theorists such as Danielson and Flerovsky provided Marx with a lot of valuable information about developments in Russian society. Marx paid great attention and provided much empathy and support to the revolutionary practice of the Russian Narodniks, who he regarded as part of the world proletarian socialist revolution. He believed that their revolutionary activities to overthrow the tsarist government would benefit both the Russian society and the proletarian revolution in Western Europe. While criticizing their misconceptions, Marx also needed to protect their revolutionary enthusiasm. Therefore, Marx adopted a relatively mild and tactical approach in his criticism. He did not publicly condemn their agricultural utopian socialism. In many cases, he criticized their misconceptions metaphorically and indirectly. The Russian revolutionaries repeatedly asked Marx to publish articles on Russia's development, but Marx declined. When he had to publish certain views, he'd adopt private correspondence to avoid open conflicts. In particular, Marx's comments on the sensitive issues of the Russian village commune and Russia's development trajectory were more cautious. Therefore, when reading Marx's relevant works, we should not just understand his thoughts literally, but grasp the true ideology and essence connoted beneath explicit words. Only thus can we reveal the intrinsic consistency between Marx's and Engels' thoughts despite their seeming differences.

3.3 The intrinsic consistency of Marx's and Engels' thoughts

The intrinsic consistency between Marx's and Engels' thoughts lies in the following aspects:

First, it may seem that Engels, rather than Marx, emphasized that the Western proletarian victory was the prerequisite for the Russian village commune to "leap over" the Caudine Forks of capitalism. This is a complete misunderstanding. Marx did comprehensively analyze the possibility and historical conditions for the Russian village commune to "leap over" the Caudine Forks of capitalism. One, Russia was the only European country that preserved the village commune nationwide at the time. Two, the Russian village commune, being contemporaneous with capitalism, may imbibe the positive fruits of capitalism without having to endure its suffering, in the transition to socialism. Three, the Russian village commune was in a historical era when capitalism was in deep crisis and would be replaced by socialism and communism, which may be the most critical conditions for the Russian village commune to "leap over" the Caudine Forks of capitalism. These conditions all imply that the Western proletarian victory was the prerequisite for the Russian village commune to "leap over" the Caudine Forks of capitalism. Having given a detailed analysis of this previously, it won't be repeated here.

Second, it is incorrect to say that Engels disapproved of, while Marx endorsed, the Russian Narodniks' views on Russia's development trajectory. A detailed and holistic reading of Marx would reveal that Marx, just like Engels, had never expressed support of the Russian Narodniks' views on the path of Russian social development. Let's see two examples below.

In "Letter to Editor of the Otecestvenniye Zapisky," Marx broadly narrated Chernyshevsky's opinion on the prospect of the Russian village commune:

> As her liberal economists maintain, Russia must begin by destroying *la commune rurale* (the village commune) in order to pass to the capitalist regime, or whether, on the contrary, she can without experiencing the tortures of this regime appropriate all its fruits by developing *ses propres donnees historiques* [the particular historic conditions already given her]. He pronounces in favour of this latter solution.

Did Marx show that he agreed with Chernyshevsky's ideas? Some Chinese would say "yes." But that's not the case. A probe into the letter indicates that Marx didn't clearly agree with Chernyshevsky's ideas; instead, he showed different views, implicitly. After narrating Chernyshevsky's ideas, Marx said:

> And my honourable critic would have had at least as much reason for inferring from my consideration for this "great Russian critic and man of learning" that I shared his views on the question, as for concluding from my polemic against the "literary man" and Pan-Slavist that I rejected them.

Next, Marx gave the following:

> To conclude, as I am not fond of leaving "something to be guessed," I will come straight to the point. In order that I might be qualified to estimate the economic development in Russia to-day, I learnt Russian and then for many years studied the official publications and others bearing on this subject. I have arrived at this conclusion: If Russia continues to pursue the path she has followed since 1861, she will lose the finest chance ever offered by history to a nation, in order to undergo all the fatal vicissitudes of the capitalist regime.[22]

On the surface, Marx seemed to be addressing other issues, which he didn't. Marx was solemnly stating that he had seriously studied this issue for years, learned Russian for it and read a lot of relevant materials, then he finally formed an independent view on the development trajectory of Russian society, which was not a bit affected by the wrong views of the Russian Narodniks. In this letter, we see that Marx offered no clear support but implicit disapproval of Chernyshevsky. To Marx, if Russia continued to follow the path it had taken since the reform of the serf system in 1861, it would develop into a capitalist country as those in Western Europe, and suffer all the misfortunes inherent in capitalism. His views have nothing contradictory with those of Engels.

In her letter to Marx on February 16, 1881, Russian Narodnik writer Vera Ivanovna Zasulich asked him to elaborate on the prospects of the Russian village commune. She hoped he could confirm whether all countries in the world would have to go through the historical inevitability of capitalism. She told Marx: Regarding the prospect of Russian village commune, "in my view, it is a life-and-death question above all for our socialist party. In one way or another, even the personal fate of our revolutionary socialists depends upon your answer to the question." Then she presented opinions of Russian intellectuals, and asked Marx to express his own opinions. She said:

> Nowadays, we often hear it said that the rural commune is an archaic form condemned to perish by history, scientific socialism and, in short, everything above debate. Those who preach such a view call themselves your disciples par excellence: "Marksists". Their strongest argument is often: "Marx said so." "But how do you derive that from *Capital*?" others object. "He does not discuss the agrarian question, and says nothing about Russia." "He would have said as much if he had discussed our country," your disciples retort with perhaps a little too much temerity … So you will understand, Citizen, how interested we are in Your opinion. You would be doing us a very great favour if you were to set forth Your ideas on the possible fate of our rural commune, and on the theory that it is historically necessary for every country in the world to pass through all the phases of capitalist production.

"In the name of my friends, I take the liberty to ask You, Citizen, to do us this favour."

> If time does not allow you to set forth Your ideas in a fairly detailed manner, then at least be so kind as to do this in the form of a letter that you would allow us to translate and publish in Russia.[23]

Zasulich's letter was earnest and compelling in its every request. Therefore, Marx was so deliberate in his reply that he revised the letter four times. His final answer was given subtly,

> Thus the analysis given in *Capital* does not provide any arguments for or against the viability of the village community, but the special research into this subject which I conducted, and for which I obtained the material from original sources, has convinced me that this community is the fulcrum of Russia's social revival, but in order that it might function in this way one would first have to eliminate the destructive influences which assail it from every quarter and then to ensure the conditions normal for spontaneous development.[24]

Here, Marx clearly stated that he did not provide, in *Capital*, any arguments for or against the viability of the village community. He believed that there were two prospects for Russian village commune: It could become the fulcrum of Russia's social revival and the starting point of communism; or it could stick to the direction wrought by the reform of the serfdom in 1861, and embark on the capitalist path as did Western European countries. He showed no agreement with Zasulich's views.

Third, superficially, Engels seemed to emphasize the possibility of the disintegration of the Russian rural commune, while Marx seemed to emphasize the possibility of avoiding the disintegration of rural commune. This, again, is a huge misunderstanding. When explaining the Russian rural commune's possible direct transition to socialism "without passing through the Caudine Forks of capitalism," Marx made it clear in (the drafts of) his reply to Zasulich that he explained it from "a theoretical viewpoint," "a purely theoretical point of view," and "a priori possibilities"; however, when he said that the public ownership of land in the Russian rural commune could possibly disintegrate into private ownership of land, and then embark on capitalistic development, Marx explained it from Russia's then reality. Marx noted in the first draft of the reply that

> [t]heoretically speaking, then, the Russian "rural commune" may preserve its land – by developing its base of common land ownership, and by eliminating the principle of private property which it also implies. It may become *a direct starting-point* of the economic system towards which modern society is tending; it may open a new chapter that does not begin with its own suicide; it may reap the fruits with which capitalist production has enriched humanity, without passing through the capitalist regime which, simply in terms of its *possible duration*, hardly counts in the life of society. *But it is necessary to descend from pure theory to Russian reality.*[25]

"From a purely theoretical point of view – that is, always supposing conditions of normal life – I must now refer to certain characteristics which differentiate the 'agricultural commune' from the more archaic type." "Both solutions are a priori possibilities, but each one naturally requires a completely different historical context."[26] Then, Marx explained from three aspects that the Russian rural commune had a dual character of both private ownership and public ownership and two possible prospects. When Marx said that the public ownership of land in Russian rural commune might disintegrate into private ownership of land and embark on capitalistic development, he put aside all theoretical considerations and discussed Russia's actual conditions. Marx wrote in the second draft of the reply,

> Leaving aside all questions of a more or less theoretical nature, I do not have to tell you that the very existence of the Russian commune is now threatened by a conspiracy of powerful interests. A certain type of capitalism, fostered by the state at the peasants' expense, has risen up against the commune and found an interest in stifling it. The landowners, too, have an interest in forming the more or less well-off peasants into an agricultural middle class, and in converting the poor farmers—that is, the mass—into mere wage labourers—that is to say, cheap labour. How can a commune resist, pounded as it is by state exactions, plundered by trade, exploited by landowners, and undermined from within by usury!

"What threatens the life of the Russian commune is neither a historical inevitability nor a theory; it is state oppression, and exploitation by capitalist intruders whom the state has made powerful at the peasants' expense."[27] Therefore, Marx's argument that the Russian rural commune may not disintegrate and directly transition to socialism was evidently made from "a theoretical point," "a purely theoretical point of view," and "a priori possibilities," on a basis of "always supposing conditions of normal life." Marx's argument that the public ownership of the Russian rural commune may become private ownership of land and then embark on capitalism was made not based on a "historical inevitability," nor a "theory," but based on "leaving aside all questions of a more or less theoretical nature," that is, from the reality of Russia at that time. Most scholars in China who studied Russia's development did not discern the unique angle of Marx's arguments and his two different perspectives on the two possible prospects of Russian rural commune. That is, the first perspective was made from "a theoretical point," "a purely theoretical point of view," or "a priori possibilities", and the second, from Russia's actual conditions. These scholars did not notice that the possibility of the first prospect was only "theoretical," while that of the second was fairly "realistic." This is the subtlety whereby many fail to accurately understand Marx. Many believe that Marx emphasized the possibility of the first prospect. In fact, however, Marx's emphasis was to warn the Russian Narodnik theorists to be vigilant against and prevent the actualization of the second prospect. There is no contradiction between Marx and Engels concerning the prospects of the Russian rural commune.

Fourth, superficially, it seems that Engels denied while Marx emphasized the possibility for the Russian rural commune to "leap over" the Caudine Forks of capitalism. This is also a misunderstanding. Engels analyzed Russia's development fundamentally on the basis of the negative passivity of its rural commune. He also emphasized that the Russian rural commune itself could not engender socialism. Therefore, whether the Russian rural commune and the Russian society would enter capitalism or socialism will be determined not by the commune itself, but by the historical conditions or the international environment it was in. After the Crimean War from 1853 to 1856, Russia had no choice but to follow a capitalist road due to historical conditions then. This has already been discussed before. Since the prospect of the Russian society and its rural commune, due to its own negative passivity, would hinge upon existing conditions, changes in the latter may alter the former. Consequently, Marx had two parallel ideas: The possibility of capitalism and the possibility for Russian society and its rural commune to leap over the Caudine Forks of capitalism. The eventual historical conditions would determine which of the two possibilities might finally actualize. In "On Social Relations in Russia," an article written 1874–1875, Engels said:

> It is clear that communal ownership in Russia is long past its period of florescence and, to all appearances, is moving towards its disintegration. Nevertheless, the possibility undeniably exists of raising this form of society to a higher one, if it should last until the circumstances are ripe for that,

and if it shows itself capable of developing in such manner that the peasants no longer cultivate the land separately, but collectively; of raising it to this higher form without it being necessary for the Russian peasants to go through the intermediate stage of bourgeois small holdings. This, however, can only happen if, before the complete break-up of communal ownership, a proletarian revolution is successfully carried out in Western Europe, creating for the Russian peasant the preconditions requisite for such a transition, particularly the material things he needs, if only to carry through the revolution, necessarily connected therewith, of his whole agricultural system.[28]

Although Engels did not use the term "without passing through the Caudine Forks of capitalism," he clearly expressed such idea. It is precisely because Engels and Marx agreed on this issue that they jointly proposed this idea in the second Russian edition of the *Manifesto of the Communist Party* in 1882. Evidently, Engels not only did not fully deny the possibility for the Russian rural commune to "leap over the Caudine Forks of capitalism," but also proposed this idea earlier than Marx. Engels proposed this idea in "On Social Relations in Russia" written in 1874–1875, and Marx proposed this idea in his "Letter to Editor of the Otecestvenniye Zapisky" in 1877. It is unfounded to assert that Engels always denied the possibility of the Russian rural commune "leaping over the Caudine Forks of capitalism." Indeed, as mentioned before, Engels believed in the early 1890s that the Russian rural commune may have lost the opportunity to leap over the Caudine Forks of capitalism. But that was due to changes in historical conditions. Conceivably, if Marx passed over a decade later, he would draw the same conclusion as Engels, as based on the intrinsic logic of the development of Marx's idea as we discussed above.

Notes

1 Marx, K. H., and Engels, F. (1987). *Marx and Engels' Correspondence with Russian Political Activists* (Ma Yiruo et al., trans.). Beijing, China: People's Publishing House. 374.
2 *An Anthology of Marx and Engels* (Vol. 3). (2009). Beijing, China: People's Publishing House, 396.
3 *An Anthology of Marx and Engels* (Vol. 4). (2009). Beijing, China: People's Publishing House, 452.
4 *An Anthology of Marx and Engels* (Vol. 3). (2009). Beijing, China: People's Publishing House, 390.
5 *An Anthology of Marx and Engels* (Vol. 3). (2009). Beijing, China: People's Publishing House, 399.
6 *An Anthology of Marx and Engels* (Vol. 4). (2009). Beijing, China: People's Publishing House, 457, 456-457.
7 *An Anthology of Marx and Engels* (Vol. 4). (2009). Beijing, China: People's Publishing House, 458–459.
8 *An Anthology of Marx and Engels* (Vol. 2). (2009). Beijing, China: People's Publishing House, 592.
9 *An Anthology of Marx and Engels* (Vol. 4). (2009). Beijing, China: People's Publishing House, 459.

10 *An Anthology of Marx and Engels* (Vol. 5). (2009). Beijing, China: People's Publishing House, 9–10.
11 Marx, K. H., and Engels, F. (1987). *Marx and Engels' Correspondence with Russian Political Activists* (Ma Yiruo et al., trans.). Beijing, China: People's Publishing Press. 612, 597.
12 Emphasis added.
13 Marx, K. H., and Engels, F. (1987). *Marx and Engels' Correspondence with Russian Political Activists* (Ma Yiruo et al., trans.). Beijing, China: People's Publishing Press. 627, 614. Emphasis added.
14 Emphasis added.
15 Marx, K. H., and Engels, F. (1987). *Marx and Engels' Correspondence with Russian Political Activists* (Ma Yiruo et al., trans.). Beijing, China: People's Publishing Press. 622–623, 643, 626, 653–654, 673, 674, 612.
16 *An Anthology of Marx and Engels* (Vol. 10). (2009). Beijing, China: People's Publishing House, 649.
17 *An Anthology of Marx and Engels* (Vol. 4). (2009). Beijing, China: People's Publishing House, 458.
18 *An Anthology of Marx and Engels* (Vol. 4). (2009). Beijing, China: People's Publishing House, 460, 461.
19 *An Anthology of Marx and Engels* (Vol. 4). (2009). Beijing, China: People's Publishing House, 463, 464, 466.
20 *An Anthology of Marx and Engels* (Vol. 3). (2009). Beijing, China: People's Publishing House, 393, 394.
21 *An Anthology of Marx and Engels* (Vol. 3). (2009). Beijing, China: People's Publishing House, 395. Emphasis added.
22 *An Anthology of Marx and Engels* (Vol. 3). (2009). Beijing, China: People's Publishing House, 464.
23 Marx, K. H., & Engels, F. (1987). *Marx and Engels' Correspondence with Russian Political Activists* (Ma Yiruo et al., trans.). Beijing, China: People's Publishing Press. 377–379.
24 *An Anthology of Marx and Engels* (Vol. 3). (2009). Beijing: People's Publishing House, 590.
25 Emphasis added.
26 *An Anthology of Marx and Engels* (Vol. 3). (2009). Beijing, China: People's Publishing House, 576, 573, 574.
27 *Collected Works of Marx and Engels* (Vol. 19). (1963). Beijing, China: People's Publishing House, 446.
28 *An Anthology of Marx and Engels* (Vol. 3). (2009). Beijing, China: People's Publishing House, 398–399.

4 The victories of the Russian October Revolution and of the Chinese Revolution do not confirm the "leaping over" theory

Another academic debate concerns whether the victories of the Russian October Revolution and of the Chinese Revolution confirm Marx and Engels's idea on "leaping over" the Caudine Forks of the capitalist system. This chapter investigates and analyzes this issue.

4.1 Proposition of the issue and resolution of the controversy

As mentioned above, due to changes in the international environment, the development of the Russian capitalism, and the impact on the Russian rural commune from all sides and varied forces eroding the Russian rural commune, the Russian rural commune lost its opportunity to "leap over" the Caudine Forks of capitalism. However, some Chinese scholars believe that the victories of the Russian October Socialist Revolution and of the Chinese Revolution vitally corroborate the "leaping over" of the Caudine Forks of capitalism. In addition, they believe such victories confirm Marx and Engels's idea that the Russian rural commune can "leap over" the Caudine Forks of the capitalist system. Such a view was proposed in the 1980s and 1990s. For example, the author of the book *The Road to Oriental Society* holds that the victory of Lenin's Russian October Socialist Revolution

> proves that undeveloped countries are able to leap over the whole development stage of the capitalist system, providing important theoretical guidance and empirical evidence for numerous undeveloped countries in the East that they can entirely leap over the development stage of capitalism.

The author further contends: "After the October Revolution, China has leaped over the whole development stage of capitalism and entered socialism. Thus, Marx's theory on non-capitalist development in Eastern society has withstood the test of practice." More explicitly, the author argues in his conclusion:

> History has proved that Russia has transitioned into a socialist society without going through capitalism; China, leaping over the entire development stage of capitalism, has embarked on the socialist road from a semi-feudal and semi-colonial society. These instances confirm Marx and Engels's idea

of "leaping over" the Caudine Forks of the capitalist system and Marx's theory on non-capitalist development in Eastern society.[1]

This view still holds certain currency in the 21st century. The author of *Beyond the Myth of Homogeneity Philosophy: A Contemporary Interpretation of Marx's Philosophical Revolution*, for example, believes that "the success of the Russian October Revolution, to a certain extent, confirms Marx's prophecy" when the author discusses Marx's vision that the Russian rural commune may "leap over" the Caudine Forks of the capitalist system.[2]

These views are untenable. I believe that the victories of the Russian October Revolution and of the Chinese Revolution do not confirm Marx and Engels' idea proposed in the 1870s and 1880s that the Russian commune could "leap over" the Caudine Forks of capitalism. I further contend that Russian October Revolution and Chinese Revolution bear no direct link with Marx and Engels' original hypothesis. This link should not be forced by ideological needs. Arguments cited above from *Road to the Oriental Society* are hampered by numerous extraneous factors. Such factors must be removed in our analysis of whether the victories of Russian October Revolution and of Chinese Revolution confirm Marx and Engels's idea that the Russian commune might have "leaped over" the Caudine Forks of the capitalist system.

First, the issues discussed here have nothing to do with Marx's so-called "theory of non-capitalist development in Eastern societies." Marx never regarded the East as a monolithic whole and never believed that all Eastern societies must uniformly follow the path of non-capitalist development. The "theory of non-capitalist development in Eastern societies" is purely fictitious. No such theory is visible in any works of Marx and Engels. We cannot help but challenge: In which book, article, or letter did Marx put forward the "theory of non-capitalist development in Eastern societies"? If Marx does offer the "theory of non-capitalist development in Eastern societies," this theory has long been falsified by the realities of many Eastern countries. Many Eastern countries, such as Japan, India, Indonesia, South Korea, Singapore, Thailand, and Malaysia, have long been recognized as capitalist. More broadly, if we include Africa and Latin America, as well as Eastern Europe and Russia, as Eastern societies, most of them are also largely capitalist. Some people want to "confirm" Marx's theory so "devoutly" that they have introduced too much imagination and subjectivity into their misguided analyses. Such misguided interpretation of Marxism does nothing other than the disservice of falsifying Marxism.

Second, the meanings of "incompletely developed capitalism," "leaping over the entire stage of capitalism," and "entirely leaped over the development stage of capitalism" remain unclear. What is "complete development of capitalism"? What is "the entire stage of capitalist development"? The author did not answer. It could be argued that as long as capitalism has not perished, then it has not yet completed its "entire stage" of development; as long as capitalism is still ongoing, its previous development is not yet "complete." The crux of the question is not the debate over "complete" or "incomplete," "full" or "half," but over the nature of Russian and Chinese societies before the victories of the Russian October Revolution and of the Chinese Revolution. If the previous society was of a pre-capitalist nature, the victories of the Russian October Revolution and the Chinese Revolution mean "leaping over" the Caudine Forks of the capitalist system; if it was already capitalist before the revolution, there would be no "leaping over" capitalism. Furthermore, whether a country has "leaped over" the Caudine Forks of capitalism depends not only on whether it is a pre-capitalist society before its proletarian revolution, but also on whether it has successfully built a socialist society after the victory. If a country is already a capitalist country before the revolutionary victory, but has not yet become a socialist society for whatever reasons and thus chooses to continue its path of capitalism after the revolution, it cannot be considered as having "leaped over" the Caudine Forks of capitalism. The disintegration of the Soviet Union and the dramatic changes in Eastern Europe force us to reconsider.

4.2 Victory of Russia's October Revolution does not confirm the "leaping over" theory

Why are the victories of the Russian October Revolution and of the Chinese Revolution not confirmation of Marx and Engels' idea that the Russian commune could "leap over" the Caudine Forks of the capitalist system? There are three major reasons.

First, the country that has "leaped over" the Caudine Forks of the capitalist system must be a pre-capitalist country. A country that is already a capitalist country will have no such "leaping over" to perform. No one would regard the victory of a hypothetical socialist revolution in developed capitalist countries such as Western Europe, North America, and Japan as "leaping over" the Caudine Forks of capitalism. This would be self-evident. So what kind of a country was Russia before the victory of the October Revolution? On the eve of his death, Engels had clearly stated that Russia had become a capitalist country, both economically and politically, as we have discussed previously. By early 20th century, Lenin had repeatedly confirmed that Russia was already a capitalist country. The idea is widely accepted and needs no further elaboration. Since Russia was already a capitalist country before the October Revolution, there would be no "leaping over" of the Caudine Forks of capitalism.

Second, according to the logic of Marx and Engels, the victory of the proletarian revolution in Western Europe makes it possible for a pre-capitalist country to "leap over" the Caudine Forks of the capitalist system. The Russian October Revolution succeeded while the countries in Western Europe were still capitalist societies. Russia's transition to socialism relied mainly on its own resources, rather than on the capitalist progress in Western Europe. Actually, Western capitalist countries jointly attacked and subverted Russia in their attempt to destroy Russia's infant socialism. Therefore, the victory of the Russian October Revolution has no direct connection with Marx and Engels's idea that the Russian commune and the Russian society might have "leaped over" the Caudine Forks of the capitalist system.

Third, Lenin said that the proletarian revolutions in economically and culturally undeveloped countries may succeed before advanced capitalist countries in

Western Europe. However, he never claimed that the economically and culturally backward countries were pre-capitalist. On the contrary, Lenin maintained that a certain degree of capitalist development and the existence of the proletariat are the basis for the socialist revolution. This basis is absent in pre-capitalist countries. If anyone claims that the pre-capitalist country can carry out the proletarian socialist revolution and succeed, the claimant would be ignorant of the fundamentals of scientific socialism. For Lenin, it is impossible to carry out a proletarian socialist revolution in a pre-capitalist country. An economically and culturally undeveloped country is not the same as a pre-capitalist country. For Lenin, a capitalist country may be either advanced or undeveloped economically and culturally. Capitalist countries with advanced economies and cultures are still a minority in the world. The economy and culture of most capitalist countries are still relatively and even seriously backward. At the turn between the 19th and the 20th centuries, when Russia first entered capitalism, the Russian Narodniks denied the capitalist nature of Russian society at the time, taking the backwardness of Russian production technology and the large presence of rural workers as pretexts. This elicited a stern rebuttal from Lenin. In "The Economic Content of Narodism and the Criticism of it in Mr. Struve's Book," he says:

> Undoubtedly, the contrasting of the Russian system to capitalism, a contrast based on the technical backwardness of our national economy, and on the predominance of hand production and so often resorted to by the Narodniks, is quite absurd, since capitalism exists both where technical development is low and where it is high.[3]

Lenin's contrast with the early capitalism in Russia and in Western Europe is very convincing. He says, in Western Europe,

> Industrial capitalism, which in its turn is at first technically quite primitive, and does not differ in any way from the old systems of production, then organises manufacture—which is still based on hand labour and on the dominant handicraft industries, without breaking the tie between the wage-worker and the land—and completes its development with large-scale machine industry. It is this last, highest stage that constitutes the culminating point of the development of capitalism.[4]

In *The Development of Capitalism in Russia*, Lenin says:

> It should be added that our literature frequently contains too stereotyped an understanding of the theoretical proposition that capitalism requires the free, landless worker. This proposition is quite correct as indicating the main trend, but capitalism penetrates into agriculture particularly slowly and in extremely varied forms. The allotment of land to the rural worker is very often to the interests of the rural employers themselves, and that is why the allotment-holding rural worker is a type to be found in all capitalist countries.

Lenin pointed out that England, France, and Prussia are all the same, but the rural workers in different countries have different forms. Lenin further analyzed:

> Each of these bears traces of a specific agrarian system, of a specific history of agrarian relations—but this does not prevent the economist from classing them all as one type of agricultural proletarian. The juridical basis of his right to his plot of land is absolutely immaterial to such a classification.[5]

It is a serious misunderstanding of Leninism to confuse the transition of the proletarian revolution of an economically and culturally backward country to socialism with "leaping over" the Caudine Forks of the capitalist system.

4.3 Victory of the Chinese Revolution does not confirm the "leaping over" theory

Why are the victories of the Russian October Revolution and of the Chinese Revolution not confirmation of Marx and Engels' idea that the Russian commune could "leap over" the Caudine Forks of the capitalist system? To answer this question, we need to clarify the nature of Chinese society before the founding of the People's Republic of China. Here we face a complicated controversy that calls for the proposition of the concept of the "bi-mode society."

In the process of social formations, due to the convergence of varied domestic and foreign influences, a bi-mode society may emerge, featuring both superior and inferior characteristics. There have been two types of bi-mode societies in history. One is a transitional type that grows out of the disintegration of the primitive society and its transition into a class society. Rural communes, such as the Asian commune, classical ancient commune, and Germanic commune, as described in the chapter "Various Formations before Capitalism" in Marx's *Economics Manuscripts of 1857–1858*, are dual social formations featuring both public and private ownerships, both classless and classed social characteristics, and elements of both the primitive and the slave societies. Thus, they represent the transitional type. Marx described the duality of Russian rural communes in the draft of his letter to Vera Zasulich. Marx regarded Russian rural communes as dual social formations, and accordingly believed that they had two possible development prospects in the historical environment of their time, which we have already mentioned before.

In human history, there is another type of dual social formation. This formation emerged when nations of lower social development were invaded or conquered by those of higher development. These nations subsequently became colonies or semi-colonies, featuring both lower and higher economic forms. The semi-colonial and semi-feudal society of old China belongs to this type of dual social formation. Colonies and semi-colonies of some imperialist countries in Asia, Africa, and Latin America also belong to this dual social formation before they gained national independence after the Second World War. That is because they were capitalist before they became colonies and semi-colonies, after which their capitalism further developed. Their pre-capitalist and capitalist economies converged to constitute their social economic foundation.

Chinese historians generally believe that capitalism in China germinated in the late Ming Dynasty. But due to suppression by powerful feudal forces, China's capitalism developed very slowly. Before its full fruition, Chinese capitalism was interrupted by the aggression of Western capitalism. After the Opium War in 1840, especially during the 1860s, foreign capitalists opened a number of factories in China. Foreign imperialism systematically cultivated a bureaucratic capitalism in China, and a bureaucratic monopoly of the bourgeoisie was formed. China thus was gradually reduced into a semi-colonial and semi-feudal society. The so-called semi-colonial and semi-feudal society is essentially a semi-feudal and semi-capitalist society. As far as its semi-feudalism is concerned, China still did not deviate from the feudal society, despite its old capitalist production relations. As a semi-colony, China had the nature of a capitalist social formation. Since China had become a semi-colonial capitalist country, a deformed colonial economy emerged. Mao Zedong's statement that "the old China was similar to a capitalist country" is justified. This statement is consistent with China's actual condition and with his correct understanding of the nature of the Chinese society during the New Democratic Revolution. He wrote in his 1947 article "The Current Situation and Our Mission":

> In the 20 years of their power, the four families of Jiang, Song, Kong and Chen accumulated huge assets worth between one and two million yuan, monopolizing the economic lifeline of China. This monopoly capital, combined with state power, became state monopoly capitalism. This monopoly capitalism was closely integrated with foreign imperialism, the native landlord class and old rich peasants, and became the feudal state monopoly capitalism of the comprador. This was the economic basis of Chiang Kai-shek's reactionary regime. The state monopolizes capitalism, oppressing not only workers and peasants, but also urban petty bourgeoisie and middle bourgeoisie. This state monopoly capitalism reached its peak after the anti-Japanese war and Japan's surrender. It prepared sufficient material conditions for the new-democratic revolution.[6]

In other words, after the old China became a semi-colony, its economic foundation of feudalism was not fundamentally shifted, and China thus largely remained a feudal society. On the other hand, as the state monopoly capitalism "monopolized the economic lifeline of the country," it became the economic basis of Chiang Kai-shek's reactionary regime. It played a leading role in determining the nature of Chinese society, and therefore we cannot simply say that China did not experience the stage of capitalism. It may be said, however, that China was under imperialist aggression and oppression, that the feudalist production relations were not fundamentally touched, and that national capitalism was greatly suppressed. Influenced by the combined forces of bureaucratic capitalism and feudalism, China experienced a stunted stage of capitalism.

By now, we have confirmed that the old China was a dual social formation with strong feudal and capitalist attributes and surely experienced the stage of capitalism. The old China was no longer a pre-capitalist society, but contained the basic conditions for the proletarian revolution. Therefore, the victory of the Chinese Revolution was not a "leaping over" of the Caudine Forks of capitalism.

Notes

1 Xie Lin (1992). *The Road to Oriental Society*. Beijing, China: China Social Sciences Press, 223, 240, 246–247.
2 Yang Xuegong (2010). *Beyond the Myth of Homogeneity in Philosophy—Contemporary Interpretation of Marx's Philosophical Revolution*. Beijing, China: Peking University Press. 202–203.
3 *Collected Works of Lenin* (Vol. 1). (1984). Beijing, China: People's Publishing House. 398.
4 *Collected Works of Lenin* (Vol. 1). (1984). Beijing, China: People's Publishing House. 399.
5 *Collected Works of Lenin* (Vol. 3). (1984). Beijing, China: People's Publishing House. 151.
6 *Selected Works of Mao Zedong* (Vol. 4). (1991). Beijing, China: People's Publishing House. 1253–1254.

5 The greatest strength of the general historical philosophy is that it is supra-historical

In his "Letter to Editor of the Otecestvenniye Zapisky" in 1877, Marx thus criticized Mikhailovsky:

> He feels himself obliged to metamorphose my historical sketch of the genesis of capitalism in Western Europe into an historico-philosophic theory of the marche generale [general path] imposed by fate upon every people, whatever the historic circumstances in which it finds itself, in order that it may ultimately arrive at the form of economy which will ensure, together with the greatest expansion of the productive powers of social labour, the most complete development of man. But I beg his pardon. (He is both honouring and shaming me too much.)[1]

The Chinese academia also diverges on Marx's thoughts on this issue.

5.1 The meaning and application of Marx's "conception of history"

Let's first look at Marx's historical overview in *Capital* of the origins of capitalism in Western Europe.

Marx pointed out in the "Letter to Editor of the Otecestvenniye Zapisky" in 1877:

> The chapter [in *Capital*] on primitive accumulation does not pretend to do more than trace the path by which, in Western Europe, the capitalist order of economy emerged from the womb of the feudal order of economy. It therefore describes the historic movement which by divorcing the producers from their means of production converts them into wage earners (proletarians in the modern sense of the word) while it converts into capitalists those who hold the means of production in possession.[2]

In the French edition of the first volume of *Capital*, Marx said:

> In discussing the genesis of capitalist production, I said that the secret is that there is at bottom "a complete separation of ... the producer from the means

of production" and that "*the expropriation of the agricultural producer* is the basis of the whole process. Only in England has it been so far accomplished in a radical manner ... But *all the other countries of Western Europe* are following the same course."[3]

Marx cited another paragraph in the French edition of *Capital Volume I* when first drafting his letter to Vera Zasulich:

> The transformation of the individualised and scattered means of production into socially concentrated means of production, the transformation, therefore, of the dwarf-like property of the many into the giant property of the few, this terrible and arduously accomplished expropriation of the mass of the people forms the pre-history of capital. *Private property*, founded on personal labour ... is supplanted by *capitalist private property*, which rests on exploitation of the labour of others, on wage-labour.[4]

Marx continued in the letter: "Thus I *expressly* restricted the 'historical inevitability' of this process to the *countries of Western Europe*."[5]

As indicated above, Marx's historical overview of the origins of capitalism in Western Europe may be summarized as follows: (1) producers are separated from the means of production and peasants are expropriated; (2) individually scattered production materials become socially concentrated, and the small properties of the many are converted into the large properties of a few; and (3) as a result, private ownership based on individual labor is replaced by capitalist private ownership. Therefore, Marx's "historical inevitability" in *Capital* on the origin of capitalism is clearly limited to Western European countries. What Marx meant was that the forms and paths of capitalism's genesis—the separation of laborers and labor materials, the deprivation of peasants, the transformation of the majority's small property into the minority's large property, and the transformation of individual small production into capitalist mass production—were restricted geographically to West Europe. Marx did not mean that only Western European countries had the historical inevitability of capitalism; that no countries outside Western Europe would go through capitalism; that they did not have the historical inevitability of capitalism; and that the Russian rural communes and their public ownership of the land certainly would not disintegrate and embark on capitalist development.

Why is Marx's historical overview of the origins of capitalism in *Capital* only applicable to Western Europe, but not to Russian rural communes in the 1870s and 1880s? We can sum up the following reasons based on Marx's relevant discourse.

First, the historical premises of the two are different. The historical movement in the genesis of capitalism in Western Europe changed one form of private ownership into another form of private ownership. The Russian rural commune, however, had public land ownership; land had never become the private property of peasants. Therefore, Marx's generalization concerning the change of one form of private ownership into another form of private ownership does not apply to the Russian rural commune with no private ownership of land.

Second, the historical environments of the two differ. In Western Europe, feudalism was dissolving while capitalism was rising. In the 1870s and 1880s, the Russian rural communes were not only the contemporary of capitalism, but also in a historical environment in which Western European capitalism experienced a crisis and was about to be replaced by socialism. Because of this, it is possible for the Russian commune not to have to endure all ills of capitalism and directly enjoy the positive fruits of capitalism in its transformation into socialism. Since capitalism was about to perish in its birthplace of Western Europe, why should Russian rural communes still take the capitalist road?

Third, because the historical premises and environments of the two are different, whether people admit or deny the historical inevitability of the transformation of the public ownership of the Russian rural communes into the private ownership of small land, their arguments for or against this change have nothing to do with Marx's historical analysis in *Capital* of the origins of capitalism in Western Europe. Marx said: "At the very most, it might be inferred that, given the present condition of the great majority of Russian peasants, their conversion into small-landowners would merely be a prologue to their swift expropriation."[6] That is, if the peasants of the Russian rural communes were turned into small private owners, it would inevitably lead to the separation of the laborers from the means of production, thus producing a capitalist mode of production. This shows that Marx's idea that the Russian rural commune and Russian society may "leap over" the Caudine Forks of capitalism does not deny that the separation of laborers and means of production necessarily leads to capitalism. In other words, it does not deny that the separation of laborers and means of production is a general law of capitalism.

Based on Marx's analysis, Marx's discussion in chapter 24 of "the So-Called Primitive Accumulation" of *Capital* (Volume 1) only concerned the historical inevitability of the genesis of capitalism, which is clearly limited to Western Europe. Marx was not saying that countries outside Western Europe did not have the historical inevitability of the genesis of capitalism. Neither did Marx argue in other chapters of *Capital* or in other works that the origin of capitalism is also limited to Western European countries. A typical research method is used in Marx's *Capital*. One country that typified capitalistic development at the time was England. Therefore, his discussion of the origin of capitalism instanced England. In the preface to the first edition of *Capital Volume I*, he said:

> The physicist either observes physical phenomena where they occur in their most typical form and most free form disturbing influence, or, wherever possible, he makes experiments under conditions that assure the occurrence of the phenomenon in its normality. In this work I have to examine the capitalist mode of production, and the conditions of production and exchange corresponding to that mode. Up to the present time, their classic ground is England. That is why England is used as the chief illustration in the development of my theoretical ideas.[7]

When discussing capital's primitive accumulation in chapter 24 of *Capital*, Marx said: The whole process of capital accumulation is based on the deprivation of agricultural producers, that is, farmers.

> The history of this expropriation, in different countries, assumes different aspects, and runs through its various phases in different orders of succession, and at different periods. In England alone, which we take as our example, has it the classic form.[8]

In addition to the typical example of England, Marx also mentioned other Western European countries such as Spain, Portugal, the Netherlands, and France. Marx's historical overview of the origins of capitalism typified England and other Western European countries, so his summary concerned only Western Europe instead of countries outside Western Europe.

However, we cannot understand Marx's statement as saying that Marx believed that only Western European countries had the historical inevitability of capitalism, which did not exist outside Western Europe. This is evident in Marx's expositions. When concluding his research on capitalism, Marx discussed the United Kingdom as a typical case. He said in the preface of the first edition of *Capital Volume I*,

> Intrinsically, it is not a question of the higher or lower degree of development of the social antagonisms that result from the natural laws of capitalist production. It is a question of these laws themselves, of these tendencies working with iron necessity towards inevitable results. The country that is more developed industrially only shows, to the less developed, the image of its own future.[9]

What Marx means here is that the capitalistic trend would extend, with "iron necessity," from more to less industrialized countries, i.e., from England and other Western European countries to those outside Western Europe. In a footnote to chapter 52 of *Capital Volume III*, Marx cited from and endorsed the German economist F. List's work "Die Ackerverfassung, die Zwergwirtschaft und die Auswanderung" (Agricultural System, Small-scale Peasant Economy and Immigration). Marx said,

> The prevalence of a self-sufficient economy on large estates demonstrates solely the lack of civilisation, means of communication, domestic trades and wealthy cities. It is to be encountered, therefore, throughout Russia, Poland, Hungary and Mecklenburg. Formerly, it was also prevalent in England; with the advance of trades and commerce, however, this was replaced by the breaking up into middle estates and the leasing of land.[10]

Marx's citation of Liszt was to show that all landed property in countries outside Western Europe would transform "into the form of landed property corresponding to the capitalist mode of production." As for other works of Marx, the historical inevitability of the origin of capitalism was not limited to Western Europe. To Marx, capitalism, per its nature, would force itself upon the world by expanding from the West to the East, and from the economically developed to the underdeveloped countries. This is fully illustrated in *Manifesto of the Communist Party* which Marx and Engels co-wrote and published in February 1848. Marx and Engels said: "The bourgeoisie has through its exploitation of the world market given a cosmopolitan character to production and consumption in every country."

> The bourgeoisie, by the rapid improvement of all instruments of production, by the immensely facilitated means of communication, draws all, even the most barbarian nations into civilisation. The cheap prices of its commodities are the heavy artillery with which it batters down all Chinese walls, with which it forces the barbarians' intensely obstinate hatred of foreigners to capitulate. It compels all nations, on pain of extinction, to adopt the bourgeois mode of production; it compels them to introduce what it calls civilisation into their midst, i.e., to become bourgeois themselves. In one word, it creates a world after its own image.[11]

5.2 How to avoid misunderstanding of Marxian concepts

To correctly understand Marx's words in *Capital*—"expressly restricted the 'historical inevitability' of this process to the countries of Western Europe"—concerning capitalism's genesis, we need to clarify the following issues:

First, we need to clarify the applicability of the above statement. As said before, Marx's discussion mainly addressed the Russian rural commune at that time and its development trajectory. It is incorrect to interpret Marx divorced from the characteristics of the Russian rural commune and its development trajectory. Western European capitalism, in its genesis, transformed one form of private ownership into another form of private ownership. However, Russia was the only European country up till then where the agricultural commune and its public ownership of land were extant nationwide. Since the land had never become the private property of the peasants, it is impossible to apply Marx's generalization of changing one form of private ownership to another form of private ownership to the Russian rural commune where the private ownership of the land was nonexistent.

Second, we need to clarify the specific pertinence of this statement of Marx. Marx's statement was directed at the misunderstandings by some Russian populist theorists of the statement from *Capital*. It is incorrect to understand Marx's thought in isolation without considering its specific pertinence, which would inevitably lead to misinterpretation. Marx's statement was closely connected with his special relationship with some populist theorists. The relationship between Marx and some Russian populist theorists was extremely subtle. These theorists believed that Russian peasants were natural voters of socialism and that Russia's lack of capitalism made Russia superior to the West, facilitating Russia's transformation to socialism. Marx disapproved of these views of Russian populist theorists. On the other hand, the populists of the Russian Revolution were particularly interested in Marx's theories and activities, and Marx had frequent exchanges with some of them, especially Nikolai Frantsevich Danielson, N Flerovsky, and others who provided Marx with a lot of valuable materials about developments in Russian society. Marx paid great attention to the revolutionary practice of the Russian populists, offered great sympathy and support, and regarded them as the allied army of the world proletarian socialist revolution. Marx argued that their revolution to overthrow the Tsar's government would boost both the Russian society and the proletarian revolution in Western Europe. Therefore, Marx criticized the erroneous ideas of Russian populists in a more friendly, tactful, and implicit way, and he did not publicly condemn their utopian agricultural socialism. Especially over sensitive issues such as the Russian rural commune and its development trajectory, Marx expressed himself very cautiously. This was done to properly handle the relationship with the Russian populist theorists. Marx repeatedly said that his statement in *Capital* ("expressly restricted the 'historical inevitability' of this process to the countries of Western Europe") concerned the genesis of capitalism. Misinterpretation would occur if we leave aside the special relationship between Marx and Russian populist theorists and understand Marx's statement in isolation.

Third, the significance of Marx's statement varied with different historical contexts. De-contextualization will lead to a rigid and dogmatic interpretation of Marx. Marx thought that his statement of the "historical inevitability" of capitalism's genesis did not apply to Russia, and was premised upon the preservation of the Russian rural commune and its public ownership of land across the country. Once the public land ownership of the Russian rural commune disintegrated to give place to private land ownership, this restriction would be gone. When Marx was alive, he had already witnessed a capitalistic fervor in Russia, and the Russian rural commune was severely damaged by forces of the state and capitalism, and was in danger of disintegration. After Marx's death, Engels made it clear that Russia had embarked on the path of capitalism, laying the foundation for the capitalist mode of production. The young Russian bourgeoisie had completely held the country in their own hands, the state had to succumb to the bourgeoisie on all economic issues, and Russia was turning into a capitalist industrial country at an ever-increasing rate. Leaving aside the changes of historical contexts and understanding Marx's statement ("expressly restricted the 'historical inevitability' of this process to the countries of Western Europe") on the origin of capitalism in an isolated way, would inevitably lead to misunderstanding of this statement.

Fourth, Marx's theory, like any theory, needs verification by practice. It is incorrect to treat a certain thought or concept of Marx as eternal truth and apply it without testing by practice. First of all, Marx's assumption that the Russian rural commune was likely to "leap over the Caudine Forks of capitalism" and enter directly into socialism had not become a reality, that is, the assumption failed the test of practice. As said before, the triumphs of the Great October Socialist Revolution in Russia and the revolution in China did not confirm but falsified Marx's thought that the Russian rural commune may "leap over the Caudine Forks of capitalism."

In addition, not only did Russia embark on capitalist development in the late 19th and early 20th centuries, but most countries in Asia, Africa, and Latin America got rid of colonial rule through national democratic revolutions after the Second World War, and embarked on the path of independent development and were integrated into the world capitalist system to a certain extent. Furthermore, after the upheavals in Eastern Europe and the disintegration of the Soviet Union in the late 1980s and early 1990s, the Soviet Union's various republics and Eastern European countries also embarked on the path of capitalist development. Under this historical context, it is inopportune to put Marx's statement in *Capital* —"expressly restricted the 'historical inevitability' of this process to the countries of Western Europe"—on the origin of capitalism—as a universally applicable theory.

Fifth, based on Marx's critique that M Shukovsky has thoroughly turned his historical summary of the origins of capitalism in Western Europe into a philosophical theory of the general development trajectory, as seen in Marx's "Letter to the Editor of the Otecestvenniye Zapiski (Annals of the Fatherland)", some scholars in China and abroad misinterpreted that Marx fundamentally denied the existence of general historico-philosophic theory. Some even believe that Marx only studied the law of development of capitalist society, did not study the laws governing the development of other societies, and did not study the universal law of the development of human history. This is not true. Marx's research and statement on the law of social development can be divided into three levels. The first level is the individual law of the development of a certain social formation, such as the development law of capitalist society. The second level is the special law of the development of certain social formations, such as class struggle, which is the basic dynamic of the development of class society. The third level is the universal law of the development of human history, including the law that social existence determines the social consciousness, which in turn reacts on the social existence, the law that the production relationship must suit productivity, the law that superstructure must suit the economic base, and the law that the masses of the people are the decisive determinant of history. Marx mainly studied the development law of capitalist society, including the law that capitalism must be replaced by socialism and communism. But this does not mean that he did not study the laws governing the development of other social formations, nor does it mean that he did not study the universal laws governing the development of human history. Even in *Capital* and its manuscripts, which specialize in the individual laws of the social development of capitalism, Marx also delved into the characteristics of various communes and formations of ownership and their pre-capitalist disintegration in certain areas. Marx's study of the entire human history adopted a reverse-chronological method. He used the metaphors of human and monkey anatomies. The "human anatomy" analogized capitalist society and the "monkey anatomy," various pre-capitalist societies. Marx believed that mastering the characteristics of capitalist society and its development law is helpful to understand the characteristics of various pre-capitalist societies and their development laws. As a result, after conducting in-depth research on capitalist society and mastering the characteristics of capitalist society and its development law, Marx made a special in-depth study on the characteristics and development laws of various pre-capitalist social formations. In his later years, Marx also devoted himself to the study of the history of ancient society and wrote five notes on "the history of ancient society," which left us a valuable intellectual legacy. This point will be discussed specifically below.

5.3 Marx's scientific attitude towards the theory of general historical philosophy

Based on Marx's critique, seen in Marx's "Letter to the Editor of the Otecestvenniye Zapiski (Annals of the Fatherland)", that M Shukovsky has thoroughly turned his historical summary of the origins of capitalism in Western Europe into a philosophical theory of the general development trajectory, some scholars in China and abroad misrepresented that Marx fundamentally denied the existence of the general historico-philosophic theory. To me, this view is not in line with Marx's original intention as based on the nature of historical conception.

As mentioned earlier, Marx's historical overview of the movement of capitalism in Western Europe refers to the concrete ways of the capitalist system of Western European countries. He described in chapter 24 "the So-Called Primitive Accumulation" of the *Capital* (Volume I) how capitalism arose out of feudalism by separating the producers from their means of production, by turning them into wage earners, and by turning possessors of production materials into capitalists. This was determined by the specific historical conditions and contexts of Western Europe at that time. It does not mean that all countries and nations, regardless of their historical contexts, were destined for this path. Specifically, Marx believed that the land ownership of the Russian rural communes, in the historical context then, may not become a system of small land ownership, may not separate laborers from the means of production, and thus may not embark on capitalist development. Rather, when conditions were right, it may "leap over" the Caudine Forks of capitalism, free from the extreme misfortunes inherent in capitalism, and directly transition to socialism. Evidently, Marx only opposed M Shukovsky's complete change of his historical summary of the origins of capitalism in Western Europe into a philosophical theory of the general development trajectory. Marx did not deny the existence of the historico-philosophical theory on the general development trajectory. As already said, historical materialism's universal laws concerning human history belong to the historical philosophy of the general development trajectory. Marx's laws on the evolution of social formations all belong to the historical philosophy theory of general development trajectory. These include the following: (1) the theory that the five social formations, including the primitive society, the slave society, the feudal society, the capitalist society, and the communist society, represent a low-to-high succession; (2) the theory of successive alternation of the personal dependence society or the natural economy society, the objective dependence society or the commodity economy society, and the society of the individual's all-round development or the product economy society; and (3) the theory of the successive alternation of the Stone Age, Bronze Age, Iron Age,

Steam Age, Electric Age, as well as the fishing society, the agricultural society, and the industrial society. From the theory of the successive alternation of the five social formations in the context of world history, the five social formations being successively replaced are universal laws of historical development. Due to specific historical conditions and contexts, certain countries and nations may "leap over" one or several social formations. Therefore, the theory of the five social formations cannot be applied mechanically to individual countries and nations.

In his 1877 "Letter to the Editor of the Otecestvenniye Zapiski," Marx compared two situations: (1) free peasants cultivating their small plots of lands were deprived of lands in ancient Rome; and (2) individual peasants were deprived of lands during early capitalism in West Europe. Marx said:

> In various places in *Capital* I allude to the destiny of the plebeians of Ancient Rome. They were originally free peasants cultivating their own plots of land on their own account. In the course of Roman history they were expropriated. The same movement which cut them off from their means of production and subsistence involved not only the formation of large landed property but also the formation of large money capital. Thus, one fine morning, there were on the one hand free men stripped of everything except their labour power, and on the other, in order to exploit this labour, the owners of all the acquired wealth. What happened? The Roman proletarians became not wage labourers but an idle "*MOB*"; and alongside them there developed a mode of production that was not capitalist but based on slavery. Thus, events strikingly analogous, but occurring in different historical milieux, led to quite disparate results. By studying each of these evolutions on its own, and then comparing them, one will easily discover the key to the phenomenon, but it will never be arrived at by employing the all-purpose formula of a general historico-philosophical theory whose supreme virtue consists in being supra-historical.[12]

Here, Marx has profoundly revealed the interrelationship between specific histories of various countries and nations and the general historico-philosophical theory. The general historico-philosophical theory is a logical conclusion abstracted from separate studies and comparisons of specific histories of various countries and nations. The above-mentioned "key to the phenomenon" refers to this abstracted logical conclusion. The general historico-philosophical theory is regarded as a kind of logical conclusion, with characteristics of "being supra-historical" and "beyond time and space," because this theory ignores historical differences and details of different countries and nations, so that it can theoretically apply to any country and nation. However, this does not mean that theory can be used as a master key and applied mechanically, without consideration of specific conditions. What does Marx specifically mean by saying "a general historico-philosophical theory whose supreme virtue consists in being supra-historical"? I think this involves the general historico-philosophical theory as opposed to specific histories of each country and nation. The specific history of each country and nation includes specific historical phenomena, events, and figures. The individuality of each country cannot represent the universality of "being supra-historical" and "transcendent of time and space." By transcending the particularity of each country, the general historico-philosophical theory promises the superiority of providing guidance with universal applicability.

To quite a few Chinese researchers, Marx's statement about "a general historico-philosophical theory whose supreme virtue consists in being supra-historical" is irony, a negation and satire of the general historico-philosophical theory. Such misinterpretation is rooted in the failure to understand the essence and scope of the general historico-philosophical theory, and the relation between generality and particularity. The general historico-philosophical theory is a conclusion logically abstracted from specific histories. By transcending differences and details of specific histories, the theory is "supra-historical" and "beyond time and space." Therefore, it becomes capable of rendering general guidance for history and methodology, and for studies of all human histories. If the general historico-philosophical theory is as specific as the particularities of each history, if the theory abstracted from Germany only has guiding significance in Germany, and the theory summarized in the 19th century is only instructive about the 19th century, the formulated theory would lose its "supreme virtue" of generality. Marx and Engels repeated that the general historico-philosophical theory, as a reflection of laws of historical development, is "supra-historical" and "transcendent of time and space." As said before, Marx instanced the capitalist economy in *Capital Volume III*, to show that the general law is only a trend and does not fully coincide with any individual occasion. He said:

> Under capitalist production, the general law acts as the prevailing tendency only in a very complicated and approximate manner, as a never ascertainable average of ceaseless fluctuations.[13]

Engels also said in his late years that none of the general economic laws "has any reality except as approximation, tendency, average, and not as immediate reality." Just because the general historico-philosophical theory is "supra-historical" and "beyond time and space," it cannot be regarded as a dogma, and must be used as a guide and method for research.

As indicated by the above analysis, Marx's criticism of M Shukovsky mainly opposed treating the general historico-philosophical theory as a master key for indiscriminate application. Marx never denied the general historico-philosophical theory itself. Instead, Marx affirmed that the theory promises guidance for specific histories of various countries and nations. The theory differs from the science of history. The science of history focuses on interpretation and description of past events, while the general historico-philosophical theory aims to obtain general principles via abstraction of the interpretation and description of specific historical processes. The relationship between the two resembles that between the individual and the general, the concrete and the abstract, history and logic, and reality and ideal. Marx's general historico-philosophical theory is actually the historical materialism he co-founded with Engels. The denial of this theory equates to the denial of historical materialism, also created by Marx and Engels and regarded as the highest achievement of human thought. Negation of the general historico-philosophical theory is equivalent to negation of the methodology whereby generality is induced from individuality, the abstract from the concrete, and general law from specific history. Consequently, the internal coherence among these will come to naught. Such negation is essentially positivism, accepting empiricism but rejecting metaphysics or theorization.

In *The German Ideology*, Marx and Engels illuminated the relation between the general historico-philosophical theory and specific histories of discrete countries and nations. They said:

> Where speculation ends – in real life – there real, positive science begins: the representation of the practical activity, of the practical process of development of men. Empty talk about consciousness ceases, and real knowledge has to take its place. When reality is depicted, philosophy as an independent branch of knowledge loses its medium of existence. At the best its place can only be taken by a summing-up of the most general results, abstractions which arise from the observation of the historical development of men. Viewed apart from real history, these abstractions have in themselves no value whatsoever. They can only serve to facilitate the arrangement of historical material, to indicate the sequence of its separate strata. But they by no means afford a recipe or schema, as does philosophy, for neatly trimming the epochs of history. On the contrary, our difficulties begin only when we set about the observation and the arrangement – the real depiction – of our historical material, whether of a past epoch or of the present. The removal of these difficulties is governed by premises which it is quite impossible to state here, but which only the study of the actual life-process and the activity of the individuals of each epoch will make evident.[14]

This section is quite similar to the paragraph quoted from Marx's "Letter to the Editor of the Otecestvenniye Zapiski," which helps us understand this section correctly. The term "philosophy" as used here does not refer to all philosophies but to abstract speculative philosophies. Apparently, in this section Marx and Engels intended to criticize Hegelian abstract, speculative historical philosophy, as well as Feuerbach's humanistic philosophy of abstract theory of human nature separated from human social and practical activities, and advocate studies into the processes of real life, people's actual activities, and actual development processes. However, they did not deny "a summing-up of the most general results, abstractions which arise from the observation of the historical development of men," and did not deny that such summing-up "can only serve to facilitate the arrangement of historical material, to indicate the sequence of its separate strata." That is, such summing-up or induction has guiding significance for the compilation of historical data. "A summing-up of the most general results, abstractions which arise from the observation of the historical development of men," is exactly the general historico-philosophical theory. What Marx opposes is the practice of separating this induction from real history, and the practice of regarding this induction as a prescription or formula applicable to discrete historical eras. Marx does not negate the summing-up or induction itself. That is, he endorses the general historico-philosophical theory.

In order to truly understand the relationship between the general historico-philosophical theory and specific historical processes of various countries and nations, it is necessary to address the relationship between the abstractness of concepts and laws, and the concreteness of the application thereof.

Concepts reflect and generalize the essence of things. In social practice, humans originally only see phenomena and the particularity of and external relations among things. They have perceptual but not conceptual knowledge of things. In the course of social practice, things that give sense perceptions and impressions repeat themselves, leading eventually to a cognitive leap or conceptualization. "Concepts are no longer the phenomena, the separate aspects and the external relations of things; they grasp the essence, the totality and the internal relations of things."[15] Concepts ignore superficial phenomena, external relations, and various accidents in the evolution of things. Concepts induce the essence of things, and thus are abstract and not fully reflective of the reality wherefrom they derive. Laws and essence are of the same nature, implying universal, essential, and inevitable relations of things and their processes, reflecting the direction and trend of the development of things. Law is stable and repetitive. As long as necessary conditions are met, phenomena in accord with the law will inevitably repeat. Lenin said: "Thus Law is Essential Relation," "Relation of essences or between essences."[16] Mao Zedong said: "'Truth' means their internal relations, that is, the laws governing them."[17] Logically and theoretically, laws generalize the process of things, giving the indirectness of thisness. Or we can say laws are not direct reality. The laws of objective things and their development process cannot be directly presented to people, and need to be grasped through abstract thinking. Therefore, laws are also abstract. Scientific abstraction is indispensable for the formation of concepts and laws, in order to reveal the essence and necessity of things. Lenin pointed out: "Knowledge is the reflection of nature by man. But this is not simple, not an immediate, not a complete reflection, but the process of a series of abstractions, the formation and development of concepts, laws, etc."[18] Concepts via scientific abstraction and theorization via objective laws should not be separated from the objective things under study. Instead they reflect the holistic, internal relations, objective necessity, and trends of things more correctly, profoundly, and completely. As Lenin said:

Thought proceeding from the concrete to the abstract—provided it is correct (NB) (and Kant, like all philosophers, speaks of correct thought)—does not get away from the truth but comes closer to it. The abstraction of matter, of a law of nature, the abstraction of value, etc., in short all scientific (correct, serious, not absurd) abstractions reflect nature more deeply, truly and completely.[19]

Please note that Lenin's concept "nature," also termed as "general nature," naturally includes human society. The word "natural" quoted above refers to nature broadly. Marx and Engels' concept of nature often implies generalized nature, including both nature and human society. Concepts and laws are abstract, but their application must be concrete, because concepts are abstraction and generalization of the essence of similar things. When we abstract and summarize the essence of similar things, we abandon the phenomenal, and the one-sidedness and external relations of these things. Therefore, when we apply concepts to analyze specific historical facts, it is necessary to combine with the phenomenal aspect, and the one-sided and external relations. Refusal to do so disables conceptual analysis of concrete things. Therefore, the application of concepts must be concrete and specific. The same is true of the law. Take the law of history as an example. The historical law is abstracted and induced from but looks beyond specific histories of various countries and nations. When we apply the law, it then becomes integrated with the specificity of nations and countries. To illustrate, here are two examples.

Example 1: General concepts and rules regarding production. In *Introduction to a Contribution to the Critique of Political Economy* written in 1858, Marx discussed the concept of "production in general." On the one hand, some believe

> it might therefore seem that, in order to speak of production at all, we must either trace the various phases in the historical process of development, or else declare from the very beginning that we are examining one particular historical period, as for instance modern bourgeois production.[20]

Marx believed this view is somewhat one-sided. He argued that it is necessary to abstract some common features and categories from the production of multifarious historical periods before studying one as a premise for theoretical research, to guide research into production of each specific historical era. He said:

> All periods of production, however, have certain features in common: they have certain common categories. *Production in general* is an abstraction, but a sensible abstraction in so far as it actually emphasises and defines the common aspects and thus avoids repetition. Yet this general concept, or the common aspect which has been brought to light by comparison, is itself a multifarious compound comprising divergent categories. Some elements are found in all epochs, others are common to a few epochs. The most modern period and the most ancient period will have (certain) categories in common.[21]

That is to say, there might be not one but several features or categories in common, which are divided into different levels. Some are common in all epochs, while others are specific to a few. Without these abstractions, no production can be derived. Marx clarified the common features or categories of the social reproduction process as production, distribution, exchange, and consumption and explained their relations. On the other hand, Marx also argued: "Thus when we speak of production, we always have in mind production at a definite stage of social development, production by individuals in a society."

> There are categories which are common to all stages of production and are established by reasoning as general categories; the so-called *general conditions* of all and any production, however, are nothing but abstract conceptions which do not define any of the actual historical stages of production.[22]

In other words, the common features or categories of all production, i.e., production in general, are abstracted from specific social forms of production by reasoning and have the characteristics of a specific social form that transcends production. Therefore, only through the combination of production in general with specific social forms of production can the former instruct the study of the latter.

The specific social form of production is the social relationship of production, namely, the productive relation. Just knowing the abstract categories of "production in general" or "general production" with knowledge of the specific expressions of these abstractions in certain production relations is not helpful for studying production under given production relations. Bourgeois economists always talk about production abstractly without considering production relations and regard capitalist production as an eternal natural process. For instance, they believe capital has existed since ancient times and will continue to exist; they hold that in any era, the means of production and of subsistence are capital, thus confusing different production relations and eternalizing capitalist relations of production. Marx was once influenced by bourgeois economists, and he called means of production such as labor tools and labor materials capital. In their work *The German Ideology* written in 1845 to 1846, Marx and Engels still adopted this idea of bourgeois economists. They said:

> The division of labour implies from the outset the division of the *conditions of labour*, of tools and materials, and thus the splitting-up of accumulated capital among different owners, and thus, also, the division between capital and labour, and the different forms of property itself.[23]

Here, they called "labour tools and materials" capital. Shortly thereafter, Marx put aside the erroneous view of bourgeois economists that the means of production of any era is capital, as seen in *Wage Labour and Capital*, which appeared in a speech delivered before the German Workingmen's Club of Brussels in December 1847, and was first published on April 5–8 and 11, 1849 in *Neue Rheinische Zeitung* as an editorial. Marx said:

> A Negro is a Negro. Only under certain conditions does he become a *slave*. A cotton-spinning machine is a machine for spinning cotton. Only under certain conditions does it become *capital*. Torn away from these conditions, it is as little capital as *gold* is itself money, or sugar is the *price* of sugar.

> *Capital* also is a social relation of production. It is a *bourgeois relation
> of production*, a relation of production of bourgeois society. The means of
> subsistence, the instruments of labour, the raw materials, of which capital
> consists – have they not been produced and accumulated under given social
> conditions, within definite special relations? Are they not employed for new
> production, under given special conditions, within definite social relations?
> And does not just the definite social character stamp the products which serve
> for new production as *capital*?[24]

In *Capital*, Marx further elaborated this idea. He said:

> Capital is not a thing, but rather a definite social production relation, belong-
> ing to a definite historical formation of society, which is manifested in a thing
> and lends this thing a specific social character. Capital is not the sum of the
> material and produced means of production. Capital is rather the means of
> production transformed into capital, which in themselves are no more capital
> than gold or silver in itself is money.[25]

To see capital as a special production relation that belongs to a definite social formation reveals the historic nature and temporality of capital. Just as its generation is
historically inevitable, so is its demise. Marx believed that not only capital, but also
capitalist modes of production, such as goods, money, value, price, wage, profit,
interest, rent, credit, surplus value, and average profit, are not things but rather the
production relations of capitalism. By perceiving all these merely as things, the bourgeois economists negated their essential embodiment of definite production relations.

  Marx called capitalist society the object-dependent society, where the object
is dominant over man rather than the vice versa and the relationship between
objects becomes a dominating power alien to and against man. The essence of
the object-dependent society lies in the fact that the relationship between objects
obscures the social relationship between people and conceals the relationship
between the exploiting capitalists and the exploited wage workers. The alienation
by the object-dependent society is seen in the following. (1) The objective conditions of labor are alienated from laborers, to wit, the materialized labor created
by the workers is alienated from their living labor. This is because the manufac-
tured products (materialized labor), in possession not of the worker but of the
capitalists, become the means by which capitalists exploit and rule the workers.
(2) Due to the materialization of social relations caused by division of labor and
exchange, social relations such as commodity, currency, and capital become a
power outside of and opposite to the producer, not serving but controlling the producer. (3) Because of the oppositions between objective conditions of labor and
laborers, and between social relations and producers, for the society as a whole,
production and exchange are presented as anarchy, and the production process
becomes a blind alien force above all labor, though the production and exchange
of individuals are carried out consciously and purposefully. (4) Owing to the
materialization of social relations between people, material production and social

relations become forces alien to and oppressive against people. So does the ideology conceived thereof. Ideology is abstract, and the oppression by ideology is also abstract. (5) In the object-dependent society, science turns into an independent force that separates from and opposes workers and serves capital. The separation of the laborers and objective conditions of labor is a feature of the capitalist mode of production. In this society, science has witnessed rapid development and is widely used in production. It is applied to the production process and materialized into production tools, that is, into fixed capital, becoming the means whereby capitalists economically exploit and rule workers. Therefore, science turns into a means that separates from, opposes, alienates, and rules workers.

Since Marx used the abstract concept of "production in general" or "general production" to study capitalist production and integrated it closely with the specific social form of capitalist production, he had a profound and concrete understanding of capitalist production, thus revealing the laws of its development. He not only affirmed the positive role that capitalist production plays, but also uncovered the nature of capitalists' exploitation of wage workers and formulated the law that capitalism must be replaced by socialism.

Example 2: Concepts and laws concerning labor and the labor process. In *Capital* and its manuscripts, Marx repeatedly mentioned the general or abstract meaning of "labor" and clarified the unity between the labor process and the value appreciation process under the capitalist mode of production. The "labor process" refers to the general or abstract nature of labor, while the "value appreciation process" refers to the specific social form of labor, namely, the social form of capitalist labor. In *Economics Manuscript of 1861–1863*, Marx said: "It is the universal condition for the metabolic interaction between nature and man, and as such a natural condition of human life it is independent of, equally common to, all particular social forms of human life."

> The labour process itself appears in its general form, hence still in *no* specific *economic determinateness*. This form does not express any particular historical (social) *relation of production* entered into by human beings in the production of their social life; it is rather the general form, and the general elements, into which labour must be uniformly divided in all social modes of production in order to function as labour.[26]

Here, "actual labor" and "labor process" indicate the abstraction of the concept of "labor." Marx further discussed this issue in *Capital*. He pointed out: "So far therefore as labour is a creator of use-value, is useful labour, it is a necessary condition, independent of all forms of society, for the existence of the human race; it is an eternal nature-imposed necessity."[27] Marx added: "We shall, therefore, in the first place, have to consider the labour-process independently of the particular form it assumes under given social conditions."

> The labour-process, resolved as above into its simple elementary factors, is human action with a view to the production of use-values, appropriation of

natural substances to human requirements; it is the necessary condition for effecting exchange of matter between man and Nature; it is the everlasting Nature-imposed condition of human existence, and therefore is independent of every social phase of that existence, or rather, is common to every such phase. It was, therefore, not necessary to represent our labourer in connexion with other labourers; man and his labour on one side, Nature and its materials on the other, sufficed.[28]

Marx said humorously that, as the taste of the porridge does not tell you who grew the oats, no more does this simple process tell you of itself what are the social conditions under which it is taking place, whether under the slave-owner's brutal lash, the anxious eye of the capitalist, or a savage in killing wild animals with stones. These are not what the labor-process is about.

The labor process, namely, labor in general, exists not in isolation, but in a particular social form and in real history. There is no labor process independent of the specific social form. Any labor is the unity of a general labor process and a specific social form. Therefore, simply using the abstract theory of a general labor process cannot explain any specific social form of labor. Only by combining the theory with a particular social labor form can the former instruct the study of the latter. Marx held that the process of production is the unity between the labor process and the process of creating value, while the capitalist process of production is the unity between the labor process and value appreciation. The capitalist production mode fuses value creation with value appreciation. Marx pointed out:

> Our capitalist has two objects in view: in the first place, he wants to produce a use-value that has a value in exchange, that is to say, an article destined to be sold, a commodity; and secondly, he desires to produce a commodity whose value shall be greater than the sum of the values of the commodities used in its production, that is, of the means of production and the labour-power, that he purchased with his good money in the open market. His aim is to produce not only a use-value, but a commodity also; not only use-value, but value; not only value, but at the same time surplus-value.
>
> The process of production, considered on the one hand as the unity of the labour-process and the process of creating value, is production of commodities; considered on the other hand as the unity of the labour-process and the process of producing surplus-value, it is the capitalist process of production, or capitalist production of commodities.[29]

Marx's examination of the capitalist production process shows that the surplus labor created by wage workers in the production process under the capitalist mode of production is the only profit source for varied capitalists, whether as profit for industrial or commercial capitalists, interest of loan capitalists, or the land rent of landowners.

Marx divided surplus value into absolute and relative surplus value. He posited that the surplus value produced by extending the workday is called absolute surplus value; on the contrary, the surplus value produced by shortening the necessary labor time and correspondingly changing the proportion of the necessary labor time and the remaining labor time of the workday is called relative surplus value. The production of absolute surplus value is only related to the length of the workday, while the production of relative surplus value causes a complete revolution in the technological process and production organization of labor. In order to increase the absolute surplus value, the capitalist prolongs the workers' labor time and intensity without changing the mode of production, that is, without changing the technical and social conditions of labor. Marx pointed out:

> Capital has evolved into command over labour, and sees to it that work is done regularly and intensively. Moreover, it compels the workers to do more work than is necessary for their sustenance; and, in pumping out surplus-labour, it surpasses all earlier production systems based upon direct compulsory labour.[30]

In order to produce more relative surplus value,

> the technical and social conditions of the process, and consequently the very mode of production must be revolutionised, before the productiveness of labour can be increased. By that means alone can the value of labour-power be made to sink, and the portion of the working day necessary for the reproduction of that value, be shortened.
>
> By increase in the productiveness of labour, we mean, generally, an alteration in the labour-process, of such a kind as to shorten the labour-time socially necessary for the production of a commodity, and to endow a given quantity of labour with the power of producing a greater quantity of use-value.[31]

Marx's *Capital* and its manuscripts are examples of combining the abstraction of labor and labor processes with the specificity of their application.

As demonstrated by the above two examples, Marx's statement that "the supreme virtue of the general historico-philosophical theory consists in being supra-historical" affirms rather than negates this theory. He incisively explained that the application of this theory must be closely integrated with reality. Otherwise, the theory is valueless.

Notes

1 *An Anthology of Marx and Engels* (Vol. 3). (2009). Beijing, China: People's Publishing House, 466.
2 *An Anthology of Marx and Engels* (Vol. 3). (2009). Beijing, China: People's Publishing House, 465.
3 *An Anthology of Marx and Engels* (Vol. 3). (2009). Beijing, China: People's Publishing House, 589. Emphasis added.
4 Emphasis added.

5 *An Anthology of Marx and Engels* (Vol. 3). (2009). Beijing, China: People's Publishing House, 570, 589. Emphasis added.
6 *An Anthology of Marx and Engels* (Vol. 3). (2009). Beijing, China: People's Publishing House, 583–584.
7 *An Anthology of Marx and Engels* (Vol. 5). (2009). Beijing, China: People's Publishing House, 8.
8 *An Anthology of Marx and Engels* (Vol. 5). (2009). Beijing, China: People's Publishing House, 823.
9 *An Anthology of Marx and Engels* (Vol. 5). (2009). Beijing, China: People's Publishing House, 8.
10 *An Anthology of Marx and Engels* (Vol. 7). (2009). Beijing, China: People's Publishing House, 1000, 1001–1002.
11 *An Anthology of Marx and Engels* (Vol. 2). (2009). Beijing, China: People's Publishing House, 35–36.
12 *An Anthology of Marx and Engels* (Vol. 3). (2009). Beijing, China: People's Publishing House, 466–467. Emphasis added.
13 *An Anthology of Marx and Engels* (Vol. 7). (2009). Beijing, China: People's Publishing House, 181.
14 *An Anthology of Marx and Engels* (Vol. 1). (2009). Beijing, China: People's Publishing House, 526.
15 *Selected Works of Mao Zedong* (Vol. 1). (1991). Beijing, China: People's Publishing House, 285.
16 *Collected Works of Lenin* (Vol. 55). (1986). Beijing, China: People's Publishing House, 128.
17 *Selected Works of Mao Zedong* (Vol. 3). (1991). Beijing, China: People's Publishing House, 801.
18 *Collected Works of Lenin* (Vol. 55). (1986). Beijing, China: People's Publishing House, 152.
19 *Collected Works of Lenin* (Vol. 55). (1986). Beijing, China: People's Publishing House, 142.
20 *An Anthology of Marx and Engels* (Vol. 8). (2009). Beijing, China: People's Publishing House, 9.
21 *An Anthology of Marx and Engels* (Vol. 8). (2009). Beijing, China: People's Publishing House, 9. Emphasis added.
22 *An Anthology of Marx and Engels* (Vol. 8). (2009). Beijing, China: People's Publishing House, 6–9,12. Emphasis added.
23 *An Anthology of Marx and Engels* (Vol. 1). (2009). Beijing, China: People's Publishing House, 579. Emphasis added.
24 *An Anthology of Marx and Engels* (Vol. 1). (2009). Beijing, China: People's Publishing House, 723, 724. Emphasis added.
25 *An Anthology of Marx and Engels* (Vol. 7). (2009). Beijing, China: People's Publishing House, 922.
26 *Collected Works of Marx and Engels* (Vol. 32). (1998). Beijing, China: People's Publishing House, 69–70. Emphasis added.
27 *An Anthology of Marx and Engels* (Vol. 5). (2009). Beijing, China: People's Publishing House, 56.
28 *An Anthology of Marx and Engels* (Vol. 5). (2009). Beijing, China: People's Publishing House, 207, 215.
29 *An Anthology of Marx and Engels* (Vol. 5). (2009). Beijing, China: People's Publishing House, 217–218, 229–230.
30 *An Anthology of Marx and Engels* (Vol. 7). (2009). Beijing, China: People's Publishing House, 359.
31 *An Anthology of Marx and Engels* (Vol. 7). (2009). Beijing, China: People's Publishing House, 366.

6 The theoretical contributions of Marx's "Notes on Ancient Social History"

Marx's research on ancient social history is closely related to, and, in our study, must be integrated with, his research on the development of oriental society.

6.1 A new theoretical milestone

Marx's "Notes on Ancient Social History" mainly refers to five notes by Marx in 1879–1882, including *Summary of M. Kovalevsky's Ancient Land Occupation, Causes, Processes and Results of Disintegration* (Vol. 1, Moscow 1979) (hereinafter referred to as *Notes on Kovalevsky*), *Conspectus of Lewis H. Morgans's Ancient Society* (London 1877) (hereinafter as *Notes on Morgan*), *Summary of Sir John Phear's The Aryan Village in India and Ceylon* (1880) (hereinafter as *Notes on Phear*), *Summary of Henry Sumner Maine's Dissertations on Early Law and Custom* (London 1875) (hereinafter as *Notes on Maine*), and *Summary of John Lubbock's Origin of Civilization & the Primitive Condition of Man* (London 1870) (hereinafter as *Notes on Lubbock*). These notes have been given different names by Chinese and foreign scholars. Some call them "Notes on Anthropology" from the perspective of anthropology; some, "Notes on Ethnology" from the perspective of ethnology; we call these notes "Notes on Ancient Social History" from the perspective of the law of human history. The Central Compilation & Translation Bureau of China also published separate editions of these notes in 1996 under the title *Marx's Notes on Ancient Social History*. Because these notes were not publicly available for a long time before and after the death of Marx, the theoretical studies that Marx did in his later years were not known to the world. Therefore, it is generally held that Marx, who had been energetic, tenacious, and innovative, disappeared from the theoretical stage and battlefield in his last years. In *Karl Marx: The Story of His Life*, even Marx's student and close comrade, Franz Mehring, a loyal follower, exponent and defender of Marx's theory, also believed that due to Marx's own health and the influence of his wife's death, he had to stop theoretical exploration in later years.

Time is the best witness and answer to the riddle of history. In 1941, the Soviet Union first published Marx's *Notes on Morgan*. In 1972, based on manuscripts of Marx's notes collected by The International Institute of Social History in Amsterdam, Netherlands, the American anthropologist Lawrence Klad published four notes written in Marx's later years, with the title *The Ethnological Notebooks of Karl Marx* (studies of Morgan, Phear, Lubbock, Maine). The second edition of the book was published in 1974, followed by translations in Japanese, German, Italian, Spanish, French, and other languages. In 1975, edited by the Marx–Engels Institute of the Soviet Union, the 45th volume of the Marx–Engels Collected Works was published, including four notes of Marx, namely, *Notes on Kovalevsky*, *Notes on Morgan*, *Notes on Maine*, and *Notes on Lubbock*. So far, all of Marx's five notes have been published. These notes indicate that Marx did not disappear from the theoretical stage and battlefield in his later years, but endured the pain of illness with fortitude. He opened up new research fields, expanded his research horizon, and carried out new theorization. Meanwhile, in the spirit of self-reflection and self-criticism, he enriched and developed his own theories, and overcame some limitations and inadequacies of his previous theories based on changes of the times and newly discovered academic materials, making his theories more scientific and comprehensive.

With the publication of these notes, a wave of research on "Marx in his later years" emerged in international academia. Scholars have various speculations and understandings about Marx's theoretical activities and purposes in his later years. Some speculations and understandings are correct, while others are biased. For example, some argue that Marx in his last years was unduly pedantic by devoting much time to excerpting"Notes on Anthropology" while his *Capital* had not been completed and published. Some argue that when the Paris Commune failed in 1871, the Western Revolution stagnated, and capitalism entered new prosperity. Marx "has lost confidence in the Western revolution and felt confused," so he shifted attention to revolution in the Eastern countries which were still in the primitive society and had more primitive social relics. Some scholars believe that Marx was trying to correct his conclusions made in his early and middle years that all countries and nations must experience the stage of capitalism regardless of their specific circumstances. They believe that the Eastern countries, unlike the West, were taking a non-capitalistic path, would be able to leap over the harsh tribulations of capitalism, and enter socialism from a pre-capitalistic society earlier than Western Europe. To me, these views are incorrect. The purpose and theoretical contribution of Marx's study of ancient social history and "Notes on Ancient Social History" in his later years were to comprehensively examine the various components of his own theories such as philosophy (mainly historical materialism), political economy, and scientific socialism, to correct deficiencies, fill vacancies, and overcome limitations of his earlier theories, based on new academic materials. Marx's "Notes on Ancient Social History" in his later years arguably established a new milestone in his theoretical activities.

6.2 Contributions to historical materialism

We know that during the period of the *Rhenish Newspaper* (1842), Marx was transitioning from idealism to materialism. In *Critique of Hegel's Philosophy of Right* written in 1843, the thought that "not the state determines the family and civil society, but the family and civil society determines the state" paved the way to historical materialism. In *Economic & Philosophic Manuscripts of 1844*, a series of basic views of historical materialism were put forward, despite traces of Feuerbach's humanism and Hegel's speculative idealism. This work shows the transition of Marx's thoughts. *The Holy Family* almost formed the historical materialism, but had not yet completely demarcated it from Feuerbach. *Theses on Feuerbach* and *The German Ideology* marked the basic formation of historical materialism, but the interpretation of the theories of historical materialism is still on the level of principles and lacks empirical verification. The capitalist society is the most complicated social organism. *Capital* has empirically demonstrated and scientifically tested the basic principles of historical materialism through analysis of the basic contradictions in capitalist society and its development trend. However, historical materialism is the science of the development of human history. What are the situations of primitive society, slave society, and feudal society before the capitalist society? Are the basic principles of historical materialism applicable to these social forms? Until the publication of the first volume of *Capital*, all these questions had not been empirically demonstrated and scientifically tested. To a large extent, the study of ancient social history in Marx's later years is to demonstrate, test, and perfect the scientific system of historical materialism through the study of pre-capitalistic social forms. The contribution of "Notes on Ancient Social History" to historical materialism is mainly reflected in the following aspects:

First, the theory of historical materialism in relation to social structure was perfected. Before writing "Notes on Ancient Social History," Marx mainly discussed, especially in *Capital*, the social structure of class society, particularly capitalism. In the chapter "Pre-Capitalist Economic Formations" in *Economic Manuscripts* (1857–1858), Marx also studied and analyzed the rural communes (Asiatic commune, ancient classical commune, Germanic commune), which were created by the disintegration of the patriarchal clan. However, people were ill-informed about social conditions before their appearance and how these communes have been produced in history. Through the study of ancient social history, especially the research on materials about ancient history provided in *Ancient Society* and other works by Morgan, Marx realized that these rural communes are not the most primitive social organizations. They were produced by the disintegration of the patriarchal clan, which in turn evolved from the matriarchal clan. The clan is the basic unit of the social organization of the primitive society. Marx employed materials provided by Morgan and other anthropologists to study and elaborate the social structure of the clan organization. To sum up, the basic structure of the clan organization is: (1) the implementation of primitive public ownership of the means of production; (2) the implementation of a collective production system of the members in the clan community in the organizational form of production and the means of labor; (3) the implementation of equal distribution of products; (4) in terms of social relations between clan members, there is no class division, no class exploitation or class oppression, and clan members are equal, united, and mutually supportive; (5) in terms of the management of clan affairs, a primitive democratic system was implemented. The whole clan society was divided into clan, fellow clan, and tribes. Later, several tribes with consanguinity formed a tribal alliance. In *Preface to The Origin of the Family, Private Property and the State* (1891, Fourth Edition), which was written in accordance with the last wish of Marx, Engels spoke highly of Morgan's research and fully affirmed Marx's research. He believed that Morgan had discovered that

> the primitive form out of which had developed the later gens organized according to father-right, the gens as we find it among the ancient civilized peoples. The Greek and Roman gens, the old riddle of all historians, now found its explanation in the Indian gens, and a new foundation was thus laid for the whole of primitive history.[1]

The relationship between productive forces and productive relations, and the relationship between economic base and superstructure constitute the social framework of class society. Whether the social framework of the class society can be used to analyze and explain that of the classless primitive society had been a challenging question for a long time. Some scholars give a negative answer to the above question. Marx believed that the family of the clan society belongs to the economic base of the society, and its system of consanguinity belongs to the superstructure of the society. The systems of consanguinity develop with changes in the family system, which means that the superstructure develops with changes in the economic base. In his book *Ancient Society*, Morgan said:

> Systems of consanguinity and ancient forms of clan organization are usually discovered together. The family represents an active principle. It is never stationary, but advances from a lower to a higher form as society advances from a lower to a higher condition … *Systems of consanguinity, on the contrary, are passive, recording the progress made by the family at long intervals apart, and only changing radically when the family has radically changed.*[2]

Marx excerpted this passage in *Notes on Morgan* and added: "And, *the same is true of the political, juridical, religious, and philosophical systems in general.*"[3] This shows that Marx believed that the principle governing the relation between economic base and superstructure of the class society is also applicable to the social structure of the clan society. The British historian Grote denies that consanguinity is the basis of the clan system, and that the clan has a common ancestor only conceptually, "the scheme and ideal basis was the same in all [clans]." Marx satirized in *Notes on Morgan*: "*not ideal, but carnal, germanice fleishlich!*"[4] Marx means that the consanguinity is a material social relationship, belonging to the economic base of the clan system, while the concept of the clan belongs to the superstructure of the clan system.

Second, it perfected the theory of historical materialism about the division of five social forms. In their book *The German Ideology* written in 1845–1846, Marx and Engels classified the pre-capitalistic history into a sequence of three forms of ownership—"tribal ownership," "classical ancient communal and state ownership," and "feudal or estate property." The second and the third forms of ownership are roughly equivalent to what we now call Western European slave society ownership and Western European feudal society ownership. Then, what would be the social form in our contemporary terminology that is equivalent to the first form of ownership? According to Marx and Engels,

> It corresponds to the undeveloped stage of production, at which a people lives by hunting and fishing, by the rearing of beasts or, in the highest stage, agriculture. In the latter case it presupposes a great mass of uncultivated stretches of land. The division of labour is at this stage still very elementary and is confined to a further extension of the natural division of labour existing in the family. The social structure is, therefore, limited to an extension of the family; patriarchal family chieftains, below them the members of the tribe, finally slaves. The slavery latent in the family only develops gradually with the increase of population, the growth of wants, and with the extension of external relations, both of war and of barter.[5]

Since "tribal ownership" has already produced slavery which was developing gradually, it is obvious that "tribal ownership" is not a "primary form" but a "secondary form" of social ownership. In other words, it is not "the form of ownership in primitive society" as we now know. Marx and Engels did not discover the form of ownership in primitive society at that time. This passage indicates that they still lacked understanding of the primitive society. They also believed that prior to the era of the clan and tribe, the clan was composed of several families. This differed from their subsequent belief that the large patriarchal family emerged after the disintegration of clans and tribes, followed by the emergence of individual families.

In 1859, when Marx summed up the general process of human history in *A Contribution to the Critique of Political Economy*, he said: "In broad outline, the Asiatic, ancient, feudal and modern bourgeois modes of production may be designated as epochs marking progress in the economic development of society."[6] Scholars diverge on which stage of human history is equivalent to the "Asiatic mode of production." As said before, people hold opinions such as primitive society, Eastern slave society, Eastern feudal society, mixed society, universal slavery society, and a special society that existed only in the East but not in the West. Before studying ancient social history and writing "Ancient Social History Notes" and related works, Marx did not fully understand the nature of the "Asiatic mode of production" and its position in the sequence of human history. In his later years, based on historical materials from Morgan's *Ancient Society* and other anthropologists, Marx explained this problem in *The Reply to Zasulich* and its drafts. He pointed out: the society (agrarian commune) based on the "Asiatic mode of production"

> as [the most recent and] the latest phase in the [archaic] primitive formation of society, is at the same time a phase in the transition to the secondary

formation, and therefore in the transition from a society based on communal property to one based on private property.[7]

This means that the society based on the "Asiatic mode of production" is transitional from communal property society to private property society and from classless society to class society. It is not the primitive society as we know today, and should not be regarded as the first social form in human history. In the preface to the first edition of *Origin of the Family, Private Property, and the State* written in 1884, Engels said:

> It is Morgan's great merit that he has discovered and reconstructed in its main lines this prehistoric basis of our written history, and that in the kinship groups of the North American Indians he has found the key to the most important and hitherto insoluble riddles of earliest Greek, Roman and German history.[8]

That means Marx discovered the primitive society in the modern sense through the study of ancient social history in his later years, and replaced the status of the "Asiatic mode of production" in *A Contribution to the Critique of Political Economy* with primitive society, thus completing the theory of the five social forms.

Third, it perfected the theory of historical materialism about the transformation from communal property society to private property society. At least the following three aspects are included in the transformation: (1) the transformation from the communal property of the means of production to the private property of the means of production; (2) the transformation from a classless social organization to a class social organization; (3) the transformation from clan institutes to state political power. We know that difference in the means of production is the basis of class division, and the state is the irreconcilable product and manifestation of class contradiction. Therefore, the triadic processes of the emergence of private ownership of the means of production, the emergence of classes, and the formation of the state are a basic theme of historical materialism based on the theories of social structure and historical development. However, in the long period of time before Marx systematically studied ancient social history and wrote "Asian Social History Notes," this problem had not been completely and scientifically solved, and was not until his later years through the study of ancient social history.

The private ownership of the means of production, classes, and states are products of clan organizations and the disintegration of public ownership of land. In *The Communist Manifesto*, written by Marx and Engels at the end of 1847 and published in February, 1848, they believed that "the history of all hitherto existing society is the history of class struggles." Marx and Engels corrected this improper view after studying the history of ancient society. In the English version of the *Preface to the Communist Manifesto* in 1888, Engels added a note to the passage cited above:

> That is, all *written* history. In 1847, the pre-history of society, the social organization existing previous to recorded history, was all but unknown.

Since then, Haxthausen discovered common ownership of land in Russia, Maurer proved it to be the social foundation from which all Teutonic races started in history, and by and by village communities were found to be, or to have been the primitive form of society everywhere from India to Ireland. The inner organization of this primitive Communistic society was laid bare, in its typical form, by Morgan's crowning discovery of the true nature of the *gens* and its relation to the *tribe*. With the dissolution of these primaeval communities society begins to be differentiated into separate and finally antagonistic classes.[9]

In his book *Origin of the Family, Private Property, and the State*, Engels explained in detail the clan commune and the disintegration of its public land ownership and the generation of classes.

In *Notes on M. Kovalevsky*, Marx excerpted Kovalevsky's account of the disintegration of the Indian commune's land ownership. Kovalevsky believed that due to the invasion by Western colonialism and the destruction of the capitalist class, land ownership of the village community in India had disintegrated. Small and large land ownerships were gradually established, and peasants were forced to become tenants attached to the landlords. Kovalevsky said:

> *Disintegration of the commune groups* is not limited to the *establishment of small peasants property*, and will inevitably lead to the large land property. As mentioned above, the *patriarchal nature* of the communes disappeared because of *capitalistic* infiltration, which has nothing to do with the commune. The influence of the head of the commune has also disappeared.[10]

Marx agreed with Kovalevsky's view and added: "the war of all against all has begun."[11] This addition is very important, indicating that the emergence of private ownership of the means of production would inevitably lead to the generation of class and class struggle, and private ownership of the means of production is the root of class struggle.

If the colonialist invasion and capitalist destruction are external factors in the collapse of the commune, then unequal property ownership due to developed productivity is the internal factor. In *Morgan's Notes*, Marx insightfully explained the internal reasons for the collapse of the commune. Morgan lacked understanding of the role of the internal material factors that led to the disintegration of the commune, and Marx not only fully estimated the decisive role of internal material factors but also the inevitability of the commune's collapse. Marx said: "That the *chiefs of the gentes*, etc., through wealth, etc. had already reached a *conflict* of interest with the *common people of the gentes*, which is unavoidably connected through *private property* in *houses*, *lands*, *herds* with the *monogamous family*."[12] Morgan believed that the emergence of private ownership had led to regional instability in the clan system. Marx revised and said: "*Aside from locality*: property difference within the same gens had transformed the unity of their interests into *antagonism* of its members; in addition, beside land and cattle, *money capital* had become of decisive importance with the *development of slavery!*"[13] Here, Marx regarded the emergence of private property, the emergence of the monogamous family, and the conflict of interest within the clan as internal forces that collapsed the clan communes.

The development of productivity, the emergence of private property and class, and increasing class contradictions would inevitably lead to the emergence of the state. Without understanding this principle, Maine regarded state power as an eternal social system that exists independently from the economic foundation of the society and the conflict of class interests. Marx criticized Maine's views sharply. In *Notes on Maine*, Marx pointed out:

> Maine ignores the much deeper aspect: that the seemingly supreme independent existence of the *state* itself is only an *illusion*, since the state in all its forms is only an *excrescence of society*. Just as the state only *appears* at a certain stage of social development, the state will also disappear when society reaches a stage of development that until now it has not reached. First the separation of individuality from the shackles of the group – this means the one-sided development of *individuality*. *These shackles were originally not despotic* (as blockhead Maine understands it) but comprised the *social bonds of the group*, the primitive community. But the true nature of the latter can only be understood if we analyze its content – in the "last" analysis, *interests*. We find then, that these interests are common to certain social groups. They are *class interests*, which in the last analysis have *economic relations* as their basis. The state is built upon these as its basis and the existence of the state presupposes the existence of *class interests*.[14]

But Maine regarded "*the political superiority*" as "something standing over society, resting solely upon itself."[15]

At the same time of writing "Ancient Social History Notes," Marx also wrote *Historical Notes*. A series of major historical events from the 1st century BC to the mid-17th century are investigated, and historical materials of European history and of some nations in Asia and Africa are sorted in the notes. Totaling 105 chapters in four books, the notes are rich and specific in content. After Marx passed away, Engels added the title *The Chronicles of the Year* when sorting out the manuscript. By utilizing empirical materials of world history, *Historical Notes* studies how private ownership society transitions to capitalism by passing through slave society and feudal society. The work bridged "Ancient Social History Notes" and *Capital*. *Historical Notes* continues and expands "Ancient Social History Notes." The work starts with the slave society—the first social form produced by the dissolution of the primitive communes. The work ends with early capitalism. Through the study of ancient social history in "Ancient Social History Notes," Marx explained the transformation from primitive society to class society (slave society); through the study of world history from the 1st century BC to the mid-17th century and *Historical Notes*, Marx illustrated how slave society and feudal society evolved into capitalist society. Through the study of capitalist political economy and the writing of *Capital*, Marx revealed the essence of capitalist society and its development trend and illustrated its inevitable transformation to socialism and communism. As such, Marx explained the entire human history from primitive society, to slave society, to feudal society, to capitalist society, and finally to socialist society and communist society. He revealed the general law of historical development and perfected the scientific system of historical materialism.

Marx's research on the whole process of human history used the reverse-chronological method—from "human anatomy" to "monkey anatomy," metaphorically speaking. In *Grundrisse: Introduction*, he said:

> Human anatomy contains a key to the anatomy of the ape. The intimations of higher development among the subordinate animal species, however, can be understood only after the higher development is already known. The bourgeois economy thus supplies the key to the ancient, etc.

"Likewise, bourgeois economics arrived at an understanding of feudal, ancient, oriental economics only after the self-criticism of bourgeois society had begun."[16] The "oriental economy" here is equivalent to the "Asiatic mode of production" in *A Contribution to the Critique of Political Economy*. As mentioned earlier, Marx replaced it with the "primitive society" in his later years. The "ancient economy" here refers to the economy of the slave society. From Marx's empirical study of human society, we can find that he did not study pre-capitalist societies such as the primitive society, the slave society, and the feudal society at first, but he studied and revealed the social structures and evolution laws of these pre-capitalist societies on the basis of the full understanding of the structure, essence, and development law of capitalist society—the most complex societal organism in human history. Because of this, his understanding of the pre-capitalist societies is more correct and deeper than the general historians' views.

6.3 The relationship between the study of ancient social history and the writing of *Capital*

Some researchers, both in China and internationally, believe that Marx's study of the history of ancient societies and the writing of "Notes on Ancient Social History" are totally separate from and contradictory to his other political economic studies and the writing of the latter volumes of *Capital*. These researchers accused Marx of giving up his studies on political economics and writing the latter volumes of *Capital* due to his undue focus on the history of ancient societies and on writing "Notes on Ancient Social History." Such accusation is unjustifiable and incongruous with reality.

As we all know, after the failure of the Paris Commune, Marx returned to his study on multiple topics. In the preface to of *Capital Volume II* organized and published by Engels for Marx in May, 1885, Engels said:

There was another intermission after 1870, due mainly to Marx's ill health. Marx employed this time in his customary way, by studying agronomics, rural relations in America and, especially, Russia, the money-market and banking, and finally natural sciences such as geology and physiology. Independent mathematical studies also figure prominently in the numerous extract notebooks of this period.[17]

After that, Engels narrated Marx's continued writing of the latter volumes of *Capital* in his remaining years. Aside from his studies on the history of ancient societies and of the world, his continued study on political economics and writing of the latter volumes of *Capital* constituted illustrious chapters of his last years. Marx's studies of political economics in his last years encompassed revising *Capital Volume I* for republishing, publishing foreign and popularized versions of *Capital Volume I* to further arm the world's working class, focusing on new movements and directions of capitalist development, and criticizing vulgar economics theories. In his last years, Marx simultaneously studied political economics, history of ancient society, and history of the world. All three studies complemented each other. An important purpose of Marx's studies on the history of ancient societies, especially the ancient land systems and the evolutions of those systems, was to deepen his ground rent theory in *Capital*.

During his studies of the history of ancient societies and the writing of "Notes on Ancient Social History," Marx's studies on political economics and writing of the latter volumes of *Capital* were not suspended. This is explicitly shown in the *Chronology of Karl Marx and F. Engels's Life and Career* (hereafter referred to as "the *Chronology*") in the first Chinese version of *Anthology of Marx and Engels*. Listed below is what Marx did in his later years as seen in the *Chronology*. October 19, 1877: Marx sent manuscripts of *Capital Volume I* to Zorge to be translated into English and informed him of needed revisions for the version to be published in America; November 1977 to July 1978: Preparation for the printing of *Capital Volume II*; May 21–31, 1878: extractions from *1st Annual Labor Report* received from the US; October– November 1978: For his work on *Capital*, read and excerpted and critiqued Paul Roth, A Chikonay, Kadi Di Hulman, L Kossa, Cha A Mann, and A Walker on banking and currency circulation; November 15 and 28, 1878: Wrote to Danielson about proposed revisions for *Capital Vol. I*, and recommended these revisions for the Russian edition of the work; second half of November–December 1878: writing Volumes II and III of *Capital* and researching on history of land relations; second half of 1879–November 1880: Critiqued A Wagner's *Political Economics Textbook, Volume 1–General or Theoretical Doctrine of the National Economy* and expressed his views on value theories as seen in *Capital*; January–December 1880: Writing Volumes II and III of *Capital*, rewrote Section 3 of Volume II, and read on political economics (landownership, land rent, agriculture, and financial issues); October 1880–March 1881: Continued to write Volumes II and III of *Capital*, extensive research on governmental documentation (blue books), and documentation on US economic developments; October 30, 1882–January 12, 1883: Resided in Venterno and prepared for the third edition of *Capital* in German.[18] The chronology above gives a sufficient demonstration that Marx in his last years, till his last breath, never ceased his studies on political economics and the revision of *Capital Volume I* and the writing of Volumes II and III of *Capital*. The assumption that Marx had abandoned his studies on political economics and the writing of the latter volumes of *Capital* in order to yield time for studying the history of ancient societies and writing "Notes on Ancient Social History" is untenable.

Let us examine how Marx and Engels assessed the relationship between Marx's studies of the history of ancient societies and the writing of "Notes on Ancient Social History," and his political economic studies and the writing of the latter volumes of *Capital*. The unique forms of Russian land relations differed from those of Western Europe, as partly evidenced by the fact that the primitive public land ownership had been largely preserved nationwide without being damaged by Western colonists, and evidenced by the fact that agricultural cultivation was done according to the principles of collective production of village community. As such, Marx and Engels gave special attention to and read extensively on the issue of Russian land systems, so as to gain a more comprehensive and accurate understanding of the issues of ground rent and land. As a result, Volumes II and III of *Capital* became classics in Russia as Volume I did in Britain. In his letter to Danielson on December 2, 1872, Marx said, "In the chapter on landownership in Capital, I intended to conduct an elaborate investigation of Russia's landownership."[19] In the preface to *Capital Volume III*, organized and published by Engels for Marx, Engels said,

> In the seventies Marx engaged in entirely new special studies for this part on ground-rent. For years he had studied the Russian originals of statistical reports inevitable after the "reform" of 1861 in Russia and other publications on landownership, had taken extracts from these originals, placed at his disposal in admirably complete form by his Russian friends, and had intended to use them for a new version of this part. Owing to the variety of forms both of landownership and of exploitation of agricultural producers in Russia, this country was to play the same role in the part dealing with ground-rent that England played in Book I in connection with industrial wage labor.[20]

During his studies on the history of ancient societies, Marx had referred to the empirical materials of the evolution of Indian village community land ownership system, to qualify and correct, to some extent, his and Engels' previous argument that "private land ownership did not exist in the east." Having been explained in previous chapters, this won't be repeated here. Failing to see this change in Marx's thought, some Chinese researchers claim that Marx insisted on the opinion that private land ownership had never existed in Eastern countries like India and China before the invasion by Western colonists. This claim violated both Marx's true intention and the actual history of the East.

In his studies of ancient social history during his last years, Marx attached great importance to the land system of each country and the diversity in their respective evolutions. He opposed using the Western European model to explain the land system of each country and their evolutions. Based on first-hand materials, Marx made a historical materialistic analysis of Kovalevsky and Phil's view of the disintegration of the village community land ownership in ancient oriental countries as being the same process as the feudalization of Western Europe. Marx concluded that the process of the disintegration of public land ownership in oriental countries should not be simply compared to the feudalization process of Western Europe in that such disintegration was not an actual feudalization process. Kovalevsky viewed the above disintegration process from a "Euro-centric" point of view, believing that the practices of abandoning redistribution of land in Mexico and Peru initiated a feudalization of fixed assets; and the disintegration of Indian village community had reached the development level of the Middle Ages in Western Europe. He claimed that the systems of public land grants to the army (fiefdom system), the contract system of public officials, and the shadowing system (attachment system) in 8th- to 18th-century India were all *"feudalism* in the Western European sense." On this, Marx pointed out,

> *At least*, Kovalevsky has *forgotten* that *serfdom* does not exist in India as a fundamental social factor! Everywhere in India, *land* belongs to the *nobility*. But that doesn't mean that land cannot be let to the commoners! Indian law dictates that *sovereign powers* cannot be *distributed* among nobles. Consequently, one major origin of *feudalism* as seen *in West Europe* was blocked in India.[21]

When exploring the relationship between family and the community in the oriental village community system, Phil considered that relationship feudalism. Marx said sarcastically in "Notes of Phil": "The fool of Phil equates the village commune with *feudalism*."[22] Why did Marx argue that feudalism in the Western European sense did not exist in India? It is because there are three features in feudalism in the Western European sense: First, the transformation of the land into manors; second, the emergence of serfs in the society; third, political diversity (decentralization). However, none of these features was seen in oriental countries like India.

Historians disagree on issues such as when and how India entered feudalism, but most of them agree that Indian entered feudalism after a process of feudalization. Professor Ma Keyao from Peking University wrote in *The History of the World—Prehistorical Part* edited by himself,

> Some Indian scholars have determined the period of Islamic ruling as the beginning of India's middle ages history, namely the 13th century. But scholars of Indian history from the perspectives of Marxism and Sharma hold a different view. Based on a large body of excavations, Sharma has determined the beginning of the Indian feudal society to be the 4th century. These excavations illuminated questions such as the emergence of feudal land system, bondage relations, servitude, distribution of judicial powers, and the formation of the feudal hierarchy. Unfortunately, his view of India's feudalism was

totally based on the Western European perspective, without adequate attention to the characteristics of India. The popular idea among Soviet scholars is that feudal elements emerged in early first century with the full transition to feudalism between the 5th and 7th centuries.[23]

However, *World History*, edited by famous Chinese historians Wu Yuqin and Qi Shirong, claimed that the Indian feudal system emerged in the period of the Gupta dynasty in the 4th to the 6th century AD and was established in the period of Harsha Empire in the 6th to the 7th century AD.[24] In view of the consensus among most historians that India had gone through its own feudalization before entering feudal society, we must cautiously interpret the ideas in Marx's "Notes on Ancient Social History": What Marx meant is that India had not gone through a feudalization process in the Western European sense. Thus, no "feudalism in the Western European sense" had existed in India. As for the questions of whether India had gone through a feudalization process with its own characteristics and whether it had entered a feudal society different from that in "Western Europe," Marx neither researched nor answered these questions.

6.4 The enrichment and development of the theory of scientific socialism

Marx's studies on the history of ancient societies and the writing of "Notes on Ancient Social History" have enriched and developed not only historical materialism and political economics, but also theories of scientific socialism. This is evidenced in the following aspects:

First, Marx enriched and developed the theory that capitalism will inevitably be replaced by socialism and communism. Marx and Engels specifically explained in these of their works: *The German Ideology*, *The Poverty of Philosophy*, *Principles of Communism*, and *The Communist Manifesto*. Later in *Capital*, they made a theoretical analysis of the basic contradictions in capitalism and its developmental trend. In "Notes on Ancient Social History," they offered a more scientific assessment of "the two necessities" based on analysis of the nature and social structure of the ancient society, analysis of the development laws of human history, and use of the dialectical methodology. The private ownership society and class society emerged due to higher productivity during the dissolution of the primitive commune and classless society. When productivity reaches a higher level, society will ascend toward and revert to public ownership society and classless society. And then socialism and communism will inevitably triumph across the world. Marx excerpted in his *Notes of Morgan* the following paragraph from Morgan's book *Ancient Society*,

Since the advent of civilization, the outgrowth of property has been so immense, its *forms* so *diversified*, its uses so expanding and its management so intelligent in the interests of its owners, that it has become, on the part of the people, *an unmanageable power. The human mind stands bewildered in the presence of its own creation.* The time will come, nevertheless, when *human* intelligence will *rise to the mastery over property*, and define the relations of the state to the property it protects, as well as the obligations and the limits of the rights of its owners. The interests of society are paramount to individual interests, and the two must be brought into just and harmonious relations. *A mere property career is not the final destiny of mankind,* if progress is to be the law of the future as it has been of the past. *The time which has passed away since civilization began* is but a fragment of the past duration of *man*'s existence; and but a fragment of the *ages yet to come. The dissolution of society bids fair to become the termination of a career of which property is the end and aim; because such a career contains the elements of self-destruction.* Democracy in government, brotherhood in society, equality in rights and privileges, and universal education, foreshadow the next higher plane of society to which experience, intelligence and knowledge are steadily tending. It *will be a revival, in a higher form, of the liberty, equality and fraternity of the ancient gentes.*[25]

Marx totally agreed with Morgan on this argument. Written near end of *Morgan's Ancient Society*, these lines may be seen as the final conclusion of this book. Engels also completely quoted this argument in his book *The Origin of the Family, Private Property and the State* and took it as the conclusion of the whole book. Marx's idea of the development process of history (primitive communist society—private ownership society—higher stage communist society) seemed to be a return to the idea in his *Economic and Philosophic Manuscripts of 1844*: humans' possession of their own idealized self—the alienation of human natures and rising of personal properties—the return to human natures and annihilation of private properties. But they only shared a similarity on the surface. Though the idea in *Economic and Philosophic Manuscripts of 1844* was a conclusion based on the analysis of economic facts, to some extent, it was also, to a larger degree, concluded through the logical deduction aided by the two crutches of Feuerbach's humanism and Hegel's dialectics, thus lacking empirical argumentation. Therefore, it is known in academic circles as "philosophical communism." However, the communist theory in "Notes on Ancient Social History," based on historical materialism and the theory of surplus value, is a scientific conclusion through empirical studies of the whole of human history, with philosophy only playing an auxiliary role.

Second, the theory of the proletarian revolutionary allied forces was enriched and developed. The issue of the allied forces of the proletarian revolution includes the following three facets:

First, the proletariat formed an alliance with peasants in its own country. When summing up the lessons of the 1848 Revolutions in Europe, Marx pointed out that the proletarian revolution can only win when supported by the peasants. He said,

When disappointed with the Napoleonic restoration, the French peasant will cease to believe in the smallholding, the whole edifice of state erected on this smallholding will collapse, and the proletarian revolution will obtain the chorus without which its solo becomes a swan song in all peasant countries.[26]

This idea of Marx was verified by the Paris Commune. One of the main reasons for the failure of the Paris Commune was that it did not receive the response and support of peasants from other provinces, resulting in French peasants' indifference to the bloody slaughter of Paris workers by the French bourgeoisie. The countries involved in Marx's "Notes on Ancient Social History" were all peasant countries, and the alliance between the proletariat and peasants would be an urgent issue for the proletarian revolution in these countries.

Second, the proletarian revolution of one country should gain the cooperation and support of the proletariat in the whole world. Meanwhile the proletariat of all countries must form a consolidated alliance. Otherwise the proletarian revolution won't succeed. In the speech delivered at a rally in Amsterdam on September 8, 1872, Marx thus assessed the experience of the Paris Commune, "This is the great lesson of the French Commune, which fell because none of the other centres – Berlin, Madrid, etc. – developed great revolutionary movements comparable to the mighty uprising of the Paris proletariat."[27]

Finally, the proletariat must form an alliance with the liberation movement of the oppressed nations in the course of the revolution. The relationship between the proletariat and the national liberation movement had always been an important issue to Marx. Early in the 1850s, he had made in-depth arguments in many articles, including the *Revolution in China and in Europe, English Atrocities in China, Persia – China*, and the article on Indian issues. In his later years of studying ancient social history and writing "Notes on Ancient Social History," Marx conducted in-depth research on the socio-economic conditions and national liberation movements in India, South Asia, Arab region, China, Poland, and other countries, and revealed the relationship between the proletarian revolution and the national liberation movement. They complemented, promoted, and depended on each other: On the one hand, the liberation movement of oppressed nations can promote the proletarian revolution in Western Europe; on the other hand, the proletarian victory in Western Europe was an important condition for the liberation of oppressed nations.

As seen so far, Marx organically linked the proletarian revolution with the peasant revolution, the revolution of one country with that of the world, and the proletarian revolution with the national liberation movement. He perfected the theory concerning proletarian revolutionary allied forces, and greatly enriched and developed the theory of "world history" that he proposed after the mid-1840s.

Third, the theory of the relationship between the Eastern Revolution and the Western Revolution was enriched and developed. During his studies of ancient social history and writing "Notes on Ancient Social History," Marx paid great attention to the relationship between the Eastern Revolution and the Western Revolution. This issue was mainly expounded in works such as "Letter to Editor of the Otecestvenniye Zapisky" in 1877, "Letter to Vera Ivanovna Zasulich" and its drafts in 1881, as well as the preface to the second Russian edition of

The Communist Manifesto co-written by Marx and Engels in 1882. As Marx's thoughts were basically consistent with and complementary to those of Engels on this issue, we should synthesize Marx's thoughts with those of Engels as seen in such works as "On Social Relations in Russia" in 1875, and the afterword to "On Social Relations in Russia" in 1894. With regard to the relationship between the proletarian revolution in Europe and the oriental revolution, there have been many studies and discussions in theoretical circles. The author has also discussed this issue in more detail in some works and papers. Here, the author will only briefly address several misunderstandings in the academic and theoretical community about Marx and Engels' related ideas.

First of all, did Marx and Engels put forward the idea of "the non-capitalist development trajectory of the Oriental society"? To some researchers in China, Marx and Engels proposed this idea in their later years. In my opinion, this view is specious. In their later years, Marx and Engels only believed that the Russian village commune and Russian society had two development prospects: (1) after the disintegration of the public ownership of land, the village commune embarked on capitalist development like Western Europe; (2) if the public ownership of land and the collective farming system were preserved, and if conditions allowed, the village commune directly transitioned to socialism, "without suffering through the Caudine Forks of capitalism." Marx and Engels never asserted that the Russian village commune and Russian society, nor even all Eastern countries, had only one development prospect (i.e., the non-capitalist development trajectory), because they had seen that countries like India, a British colony, had gradually embarked on the path of capitalism; in Russia, the "mania of capitalism" had "prevailed rapidly." The idea of "the non-capitalist development trajectory of the Oriental society" is entirely a "misconception" which some people "attach under the name of Marxism."

What's the fact? Did Marx and Engels deny the theory proposed in their early and middle years—as dictated by the general law of the development of human history, pre-capitalist countries have to go through capitalism before their transformation into socialism and communism? Some people in Chinese theoretical circles have misunderstood Marx's views like "the 'historical inevitability' of the origin of capitalism" "is expressly limited to countries of Western Europe" which he quoted from the *Capital*, and wrote in the "Letter to Editor of the Otecestvenniye Zapisky," the "Letter to Vera Ivanovna Zasulich," and its drafts. In fact, only the specific forms of the origin of capitalism in England, as Marx and Engels summarized in chapter 24 "the So-Called Primitive Accumulation" of *Capital* (Volume I), were "limited to the countries of Western Europe." This, however, doesn't mean that only countries within, rather than those outside, Western Europe had the historical inevitability of embarking on capitalism. In fact, Marx and Engels believed that pre-capitalist countries can directly enter socialism without going through capitalism only under particular historical conditions. According to the general law, pre-capitalist countries such as Russia could only embark on the capitalist path after the disintegration of the village commune and the public ownership of land. Marx and Engels did not change this view even in their later years. It becomes evident with a careful reading of their later works.

Next, how to interpret Marx on this view, "which of the two development prospects of the Russian village commune and Russian society would come true depended on Russia's 'historical environment'"? Many Chinese scholars give a one-sided understanding of Russia's "historical environment." They only see that Russia at that time was contemporaneous with Western European capitalism, and thus may have enjoyed the direct fruits of capitalism without having to suffer the torments of capitalism. However, they ignore another idea repeatedly emphasized by Marx, which is that the Russian village commune and Russian society were in the historical era where capitalism was in crisis and would be replaced by socialism and communism. The latter condition can be said to be the most fundamental historical condition for the Russian village commune and Russian society to "leap over the Caudine Forks of capitalism" and directly transition to a socialist society.

Finally, did Marx and Engels put forward the idea that economically and culturally backward countries would first break out with and win the proletarian socialist revolution? In the "Letter to Vera Ivanovna Zasulich" and its drafts, Marx wrote: "To save the Russian commune, a Russian revolution is necessary." To some researchers, Marx's "Russian revolution" referred to a proletarian socialist revolution, so they conclude that Russia, with its economic and cultural backwardness, may win the proletarian socialist revolution before Western Europe. They also argue that this idea was proposed by Marx and Engels in their later years. All such are misinterpretations of Marx and Engels. In fact, the "Russian revolution" Marx spoke of did not refer to a proletarian socialist revolution, but to the revolution of the Russian Narodniks and the Narodnaya Volya to overthrow the Tsarist government. Marx and Engels had always believed that the victory of the proletarian revolution in Western Europe was the prerequisite for the economically and culturally backward country to "leap over the Caudine Forks of capitalism." Marx and Engels never raised the idea that the proletarian socialist revolution would erupt and succeed first in backward countries.

Notes

1 *An Anthology of Marx and Engels* (Vol. 4). (2009). Beijing, China: People's Publishing House, 28.
2 Emphasis added.
3 *Collected Works of Marx and Engels* (Vol. 45). (1985). Beijing, China: People's Publishing House, 353, 354. Emphasis added.
4 *Collected Works of Marx and Engels* (Vol. 45). (1985). Beijing, China: People's Publishing House, 503. Emphasis added.
5 *An Anthology of Marx and Engels* (Vol. 1). (2009). Beijing, China: People's Publishing House, 521.
6 *An Anthology of Marx and Engels* (Vol. 2). (2009). Beijing, China: People's Publishing House, 592.
7 *An Anthology of Marx and Engels* (Vol. 3). (2009). Beijing, China: People's Publishing House, 586.

 8 *An Anthology of Marx and Engels* (Vol. 4). (2009). Beijing, China: People's Publishing House, 16.
 9 *An Anthology of Marx and Engels* (Vol. 2). (2009). Beijing, China: People's Publishing House, 31. Emphasis added.
10 Emphasis added.
11 *Collected Works of Marx and Engels* (Vol. 45). (1985). Beijing, China: People's Publishing House, 304.
12 *Collected Works of Marx and Engels* (Vol. 45). (1985). Beijing, China: People's Publishing House, 517. Emphasis added.
13 *Collected Works of Marx and Engels* (Vol. 45). (1985). Beijing, China: People's Publishing House, 522. Emphasis added.
14 Emphasis added.
15 *Collected Works of Marx and Engels* (Vol. 45). (1985). Beijing, China: People's Publishing House, 646–647. Emphasis added.
16 *An Anthology of Marx and Engels* (Vol. 8). (2009). Beijing, China: People's Publishing House, 29, 30.
17 *An Anthology of Marx and Engels* (Vol. 6). (2009). Beijing, China: People's Publishing House, 7.
18 *Collected Works of Marx and Engels* (Vol. 19). (1963). Beijing, China: People's Publishing House, 672–694.
19 *Collected Works of Marx and Engels* (Vol. 33). (1973). Beijing, China: People's Publishing House, 549.
20 *An Anthology of Marx and Engels* (Vol. 7). (2009). Beijing, China: People's Publishing House, 10–11.
21 *Collected Works of Marx and Engels* (Vol. 45). (1985). Beijing, China: People's Publishing House, 284, 274. Emphasis added.
22 Central Compilation and Translation Bureau (Ed.) (1996). *Notes on Marx's Ancient Social History*. Beijing, China: People's Publishing House, 385. Emphasis added.
23 Ma Keyao (Ed.). (1989). *History of World Civilization—Medieval Times*. Beijing, China: Peking University Press, 64.
24 Wu Yuqin & Qi Shirong (Eds.). (1994). *World History—Ancient History Series*. Beijing, China: Higher Education Press, 81–94.
25 *Collected Works of Marx and Engels* (Vol. 45). (1985). Beijing, China: People's Publishing House, 397–398. Emphasis added.
26 *Collected Works of Marx and Engels* (Vol. 8). (1961). Beijing, China: People's Publishing House, 665.
27 *Collected Works of Marx and Engels* (Vol. 18). (1964). Beijing, China: People's Publishing House, 180.

Bibliography

Classic works of Marxism

1. *An Anthology of Marx and Engels* (Vols. 1–10). (2009). Beijing, China: People's Publishing House.
2. *Collected Works of Lenin* (Vol. 1). (1984). Beijing, China: People's Publishing House.
3. *Collected Works of Lenin* (Vol. 10). (1987). Beijing, China: People's Publishing House.
4. *Collected Works of Lenin* (Vol. 11). (1987). Beijing, China: People's Publishing House.
5. *Collected Works of Lenin* (Vol. 12). (1987). Beijing, China: People's Publishing House.
6. *Collected Works of Lenin* (Vol. 32). (1985). Beijing, China: People's Publishing House.
7. *Collected Works of Lenin* (Vol. 33). (1985). Beijing, China: People's Publishing House.
8. *Collected Works of Lenin* (Vol. 34). (1985). Beijing, China: People's Publishing House.
9. *Collected Works of Lenin* (Vol. 35). (1985). Beijing, China: People's Publishing House.
10. *Collected Works of Lenin* (Vol. 36). (1985). Beijing, China: People's Publishing House.
11. *Collected Works of Lenin* (Vol. 37). (1986). Beijing, China: People's Publishing House.
12. *Collected Works of Lenin* (Vol. 38).(1986). Beijing, China: People's Publishing House.
13. *Collected Works of Lenin* (Vol. 40). (1986). Beijing, China: People's Publishing House.
14. *Collected Works of Lenin* (Vol. 41). (1986). Beijing, China: People's Publishing House.
15. *Collected Works of Lenin* (Vol. 42). (1987). Beijing, China: People's Publishing House.
16. *Collected Works of Lenin* (Vol. 43). (1987). Beijing, China: People's Publishing House.
17. *Collected Works of Lenin* (Vol. 55). (1990). Beijing, China: People's Publishing House.
18. *Collected Works of Marx and Engels* (Vol. 1). (1955). Beijing, China: People's Publishing House.

19. *Collected Works of Marx and Engels* (Vol. 3). (1960). Beijing, China: People's Publishing House.
20. *Collected works of Marx and Engels* (Vol. 19). (1963). Beijing, China: People's Publishing House.
21. *Collected Works of Marx and Engels* (Vol. 20). (1971). Beijing, China: People's Publishing House.
22. *Collected Works of Marx and Engels* (Vol. 28). (1973). Beijing, China: People's Publishing House.
23. *Collected Works of Marx and Engels* (Vol. 32). (1974). Beijing, China: People's Publishing House.
24. *Collected Works of Marx and Engels* (Vol. 33). (1973). Beijing, China: People's Publishing House.
25. *Collected Works of Marx and Engels* (Vol. 35). (1971). Beijing, China: People's Publishing House.
26. *Collected Works of Marx and Engels* (Vol. 39). (1974). Beijing, China: People's Publishing House.
27. *Collected Works of Marx and Engels* (Vol. 1). (1995). Beijing, China: People's Publishing House.
28. *Collected Works of Marx and Engels* (Vol. 3). (2002). Beijing, China: People's Publishing House.
29. *Collected Works of Marx and Engels* (Vol. 21). (2003). Beijing, China: People's Publishing House.
30. *Collected Works of Marx and Engels* (Vol. 30). (1995). Beijing, China: People's Publishing House.
31. *Collected Works of Marx and Engels* (Vol. 31). (1998). Beijing, China: People's Publishing House.
32. *Collected Works of Marx and Engels* (Vol. 32). (1998). Beijing, China: People's Publishing House.
33. *Collected Works of Marx and Engels* (Vol. 33). (2004). Beijing, China: People's Publishing House.
34. *Collected Works of Marx and Engels* (Vol. 34). (2008). Beijing, China: People's Publishing House.
35. *Collected Works of Stalin* (Vol. 8). (1954). Beijing, China: People's Publishing House.
36. *Selected Works of Lenin* (Vols. 1–4). (1995). Beijing, China: People's Publishing House.
37. *Selected Works of Marx and Engels* (Vols. 1–4). (1995). Beijing, China: People's Publishing House.
38. *Selected Works of Stalin* (Vols. 1–2). (1972). Beijing, China: People's Publishing House.

Chinese literature

39. Ailin Luo (2007). *Research on Rural Communities in the Late Feudal Society of Russia*. Guilin, China: Guangxi Normal University Press.
40. Central Compilation and Translation Bureau & International Communist Movement History Research Office. (Ed.). (1983). *Russian Populist Anthology*. Beijing, China: People's Publishing House.

41. Central Compilation and Translation Bureau (Ed.) (1996). *Notes on Marx's Ancient Social History*. Beijing, China: People's Publishing House.
42. Editing Group of *History of the International Communist Movement*. (2012). *History of the International Communist Movement*. Beijing, China: People's Publishing House and Higher Education Press.
43. Gang Feng (1992). *Non-western Theory of Social Development and Marx*. Zhejiang, China: Zhejiang People's Publishing House.
44. Huan Zhu (Ed.) (1996). *A Comparative Study on the Feudal Economic Forms of Asia and Europe*. Changchun, China: Northeast Normal University Press.
45. Jianjin Zhu (1996). *Where Does the Eastern Society Go—Marx's Theory of the Eastern Society*. Shanghai, China: Shanghai Academy of Social Sciences Press.
46. Keyao Ma (Ed.). (2004) *History of World civilization* (Vols. 1–2). Beijing, China: Peking University Press.
47. Liangzao Yu (2011). *Marx's Orientalism*. Beijing, China: People's Publishing House.
48. Liangzao Yu & Xu Qin (2015). *Classical Works and Fundamental Theories on Social Development in Eastern Backward Countries*. Beijing, China: People's Publishing House.
49. Lin Xie (1992). *The Road to Oriental Society*. Beijing, China: China Social Sciences Press.
50. Longhua Zhu (1991). *World History—Ancient Part*. Beijing, China: Peking University Press.
51. Publicity Department of the Central Committee of the Communist Party (Ed.) (2014). *World Socialism: 500 Years (Party Cadre Reader)*. Beijing, China: Party Building Readings Publishing House and Learning Press.
52. Qiliang, Liu (1994). *Marx's Theory of the Oriental Society*. Shanghai, China: Xuelin Press.
53. Weian Cao (2002). *The New Theory of Russian History—Basic Issues Affecting the Development of Russian History*. Beijing, China: China Social Sciences Press.
54. Xianda Chen (1987). *Going Deep in History—A Study of Marx's Concept of History*. Shanghai, China: Shanghai People's Publishing House.
55. Xingpei Yuan et al. (2013). *Marx and Engels on the "Oriental Village Community": A Research Reader*. Beijing, China: Central Compilation & Translation Press.
56. Yan Jin & Qin Hui (2013). *Rural Commune, Reform and Revolution—Village Community Tradition and the Road to Russian Modernization*. Beijing, China: The Eastern Publishing Co., Ltd.
57. Yifan Zheng (Ed.) (2008). *An Introductory Reader to Trotsky*. Beijing, China: Central Compilation & Translation Press.
58. Yue Lu et al. (1992). *The Creative Exploration of Marx in his Later Years—On "Anthropological Notes"*. Zhengzhou, China: Henan People's Publishing House.
59. Yunlong Zhang (2001). *Crossing the "Forks"—Marx's Thoughts in his Later Years and the Theory of Contemporary Social Development*. Beijing, China: People's Publishing House.
60. Yuqin Wu & Qi Shirong (Eds.) (1994). *World History—Ancient History Series*. Beijing, China: Higher Education Press.
61. Zhenhua Hao (Ed.) (1981). *Foreign Scholars on the Asiatic Mode of Production* (Vols. 1–2). Beijing, China: China Social Sciences Press.

94 *Bibliography*

Other literature: translations

62. Appianus, A. (1976). *Roman History* (Vols. 1–2) (Xie Defeng Trans.). Beijing, China: The Commercial Press.
63. Bentley, J., & Ziegler, H. (2007). *Traditions & Encounters* (Vols. 1–2, 3rd ed.) (Wei Fenglian et al. Trans.). Beijing, China: Peking University Press.
64. Flerovsky, E. (Bervi,V. V.) (1994). *The Condition of the Working Class in Russia* (Chen Ruiming Trans.). Beijing, China: The Commercial Press.
65. Hegel, G. W. F. (1956). *Historical Philosophy* (Wang Zaoshi Trans.). Shanghai, China: SDX Joint Publishing Company.
66. Marx, K. H., & Engels, F. (1987). *Marx and Engels' Correspondence with Russian Political Activists* (Ma Yiruo et al., Trans.). Beijing, China: People's Publishing Press.
67. Melotti, U. (1981). *Marx and the Third World* (Gao Xian et al., Trans.). Beijing, China: The Commercial Press.
68. Morgan, L. H. (1977). *Ancient Society* (Vols. 1–2) (Yang Dongchun Trans.). Beijing, China: The Commercial Press.
69. Rousseau, J. J. (2009). *On the Origin of Human Inequality* (Lü Zhuo Trans.). Beijing, China: China Social Sciences Press.
70. Rousseau, J. J. (2009). *The Social Contract* (Xu Qiang Trans.). Beijing, China: China Social Sciences Press.
71. Stavrianos, L. S. (2005). *A Global History–From Prehistory to the 21st Century* (Vols. 1–2, 7th edition) (Dong Shuhui et al., Trans.). Beijing, China: Peking University Press.
72. Thucydides, A. (1960). *History of the Peloponnesian War* (Vols. 1–2) (Xie Defeng Trans.). Beijing, China: The Commercial Press.
73. Toynbee, A. (1964). *A Study of History* (Vols. 1–3) (Cao Mofeng et al., Trans.). Shanghai, China: Shanghai People's Publishing House.
74. Trotsky, L. (2014). *The History of the Russian Revolution* (Vols. 1–3) (Ding Duben Trans.). Beijing, China: The Commercial Press.

Index